Biscuit Rules

Homemade is the gold standard for the *Biscuit Dive Guide*. Any Southern kitchen featured in this book turns out biscuits made the Southern way, from scratch – no shortcuts.

Follow the Biscuit Blog at
www.theriseofthesouthernbiscuit.com.

*Carol Fay and Filmmaker/Author Maryann Byrd with
biscuits and awards for the documentary*
The Rise of the Southern Biscuit.

THE BISCUIT DIVE GUIDE

Restaurants & Recipes

By
Maryann Byrd

Get your biscuit fix at:
www.theriseofthesouthernbiscuit.com

Vintage Labels provided by the Tennessee State Library Archives

Revised February 2010

Printed in the United States of America on acid-free paper.

ISBN 10 digit: 1-4243-0587-X
ISBN 13-digit: 978-1-4243-0587-2

Original layout and interior design by Westview Publishing Co., Inc.

Layout revisions and cover design by Hugh Daniel, hpdDesign.com

Cover photograph by Maryann Byrd

For more biscuit news and recipes go to
www.theriseofthesouthernbiscuit.com

To my Father, Richard Byrd – gifted with Southern charm and insight into what really matters – a biscuit lover if there ever was one. Biscuits and gravy to be exact. For him—the two went hand in hand. My dad enjoyed simple expressions of love, like biscuits. I carried him in my heart on my biscuit journey. I saw his loving spirit in the biscuit makers I interviewed and in the smiles of the biscuit fans I met along the way. They, just like my dad—and now like me— understand the magic of the Southern biscuit.

Special Thanks

Special thanks to Beth Curley President and CEO of Nashville Public Television. Beth, there have been many biscuits eaten and words written since hats, cigars, and a funky place called the Frothy Monkey! Thank you for your vigilance in promoting independent producers who, like you and PBS, believe in quality television. My heartfelt thanks go to my friends and colleagues: Justin Harvey, Jim Demarco, and Ed Jones, Mike Lewis and dear friend and videographer Michael Dennis.

Passing biscuits to the left at Monell's in Nashville.

Thinly sliced country ham on angel biscuits sold at G & W Hamery in Murfreesboro, Tennessee.

A Tennessee County Ham Festival

Bob Woods and his Country Ham

Contents

Biscuit Thanks

I've met some memorable and interesting people in my career as a journalist. Yet, the biscuit makers I interviewed for the Emmy Award Winning documentary *The Rise of the Southern Biscuit*, and for *The Biscuit Dive Guide*, have captured my heart. Each of you is so genuine, fun loving, and kind. Thank you for sharing your love of the Southern biscuit, your recipes, baking secrets—and more so for letting me taste them!

Thank you: Don Luna, Delia Champion, Scott Peacock, Edna Lewis, Lynn Winter, Mother Mildred, Lanora Reese, Carol Fay, Bert & Felix, Phila Hach, Miss Daisy King, Jeff Brakebill, Martha Phelps Stamp, Pauline Brown, Bret Clack, Pat Morgan, Bob Light, Sema Wilkes, Rob Atherholt, Paula Dean, Lou Lockicchio, Mildred Shaw, Jim Gerhardt, Michael Cunha, Kathy Carry, Chad McGuire, Bill Tudor, Shirley Dowell, Daddy Frank, Fred Simonson, Regina Charboneau, Peter Trosclar, Lanny Brasher, Martha Margiotis, Bob Henry, Mike Richmond, Phil Bryant, Pam Hardin, Sharron Johnson, Gary Patton, Marilyn Kreider, Janet Garner, Lynn Tolley, Michael King, Norma Manis, Eydie Pryor, Cecil & Janet Schmidt, Mark Chapman, Belinda Kemper, Melinda Henderson, William Webb, Sarah Woods, Brian Uhl, Robert Stehling, John Stehling, Robert Stehling Sr., Nicole Anhalt, Sheree McDowell, and E.C. Warren, Bob Woods and John Colson.

Biscuit Introduction

I live in Music City—Nashville Tennessee—where I can drive 10 to 40 minutes from my office and have some of the best and unique homemade Southern biscuits at my fingertips. Lips to be more accurate. I didn't realize what a treat that was until took on the project of this book; Finding café's and restaurants that still make the homemade biscuit. It was quite a task. Tasty and enjoyable for sure. But you'd be surprised how many "Southern" restaurants cheat and serve frozen biscuits—fooling many customers who assume they're tasting homemade. Now, some frozen biscuits are good, so bigger crimes have been committed—for sure. But nothing replaces a traditional homemade biscuit.

Now, if you've opened this book, you must be into biscuits - the idea of them, the taste of them, or baking them. You have come to the right place because *The Biscuit Dive Guide* is your roadmap to Southern biscuit making and biscuit eating joy.

This book is a companion to the Emmy Award Winning PBS documentary, *The Rise of the Southern Biscuit*, where we learn that a biscuit is not just a biscuit. They're personal. Every biscuit maker has his or her own technique for creating an unforgettable memory. And you can too.

So what makes a Southern biscuit "Southern?" Most of us from the South would smile and reply, "It takes a Southerner to make a Southern biscuit." No two Southerners are alike and neither are our biscuits. The good news is; we love sharing our biscuit tradition – so even a "non-Southerner" can adopt the Southern charm of biscuit making. My favorite quote in the documentary is; "Love and biscuits belong in every home." Phila Hach said that—and that is how many Southerners feel about the homemade biscuit.

Phila Hach is a noted Southern Chef and cookbook author. She spent hours baking a variety of biscuits for me while filming ***The Rise of the Southern Biscuit***. Phila, who often teaches new brides how to make biscuits, says "You can give five brides the same ingredients and watch them use the exact same mixing and rolling technique, and you'll get five different tasting biscuits out of the oven." That is the wonderful thing about the Southern biscuit – the personal touch. Biscuits are as individual as fingerprints.

Some biscuit makers swear the temperature of the hands and the pressure applied to the dough affects these floury creations. No matter the reason, so many Southerners have told me, "No one makes biscuits like my Mom or my Grandma." No one can or ever will because you can't duplicate "touch" and the personal choice of ingredients that make up the individuality of the Southern biscuit.

In this book you will find biscuits made with lard, butter, shortening, mayonnaise, European margarine, sour cream, and heavy cream. Some biscuit makers blend combinations of fats to create their outcome. Biscuits in these pages are laced with bacon fat, jalapenos, cheese, sugar, honey, corn, chili powder, onion, garlic, sweet potatoes, and bourbon mash. The dough is blended with buttermilk, whole milk, light cream, skim milk, heavy cream, and good old H2o.
 Some say knead it, and others fold it; some say barely touch it, pat it, or roll it. Some advise to cut the biscuits big, cut

them not so big, cut them in squares, make them tall, or make them small!

The point is: A Southern biscuit is what you choose to make it. If it's homemade and made with love you can't go wrong. As Executive Chef Scott Peacock says, "Even if you make a bad homemade biscuit it is still pretty good!" He's right.

The Biscuit Dive Guide serves a dual purpose. Use it as a "guide" as you travel to find the best Southern cafés, diners, and restaurants that still make biscuits from scratch - the Southern way. Also, use the ***Dive Guide*** as a cookbook – as many of the biscuit makers we met along the way took time from their biscuit making to share their recipes and secrets on how to make a successful biscuit.

Beaten biscuits were often served in Southern high society.
These are vintage labels from favorite brands.

Biscuit Wisdom

It is part of the human condition to want to be liked, admired, and remembered. If you desire these things – my recommendation – is to learn how to make a simple homemade Southern biscuit. You will be remembered. I happened upon this truth while researching and filming the documentary, ***The Rise of the Southern Biscuit***. The biscuit makers I came to know were the most popular, well-liked people I've ever met. I'm here to tell you it's the biscuits!

Something magical happens when you mix the selflessness of making something homemade with the positive memories attached to this icon of Southern hospitality. It's a winning recipe for friendship and love. The biscuit eaters I talked with would light up as they tasted a biscuit and fondly remembered the one who used to bake biscuits for them. Mom came in first with grandma a close second.

Homemade biscuits take time and trouble – and those on the receiving end feel special and like they matter – a feeling that's never forgotten. That effort is the hook on which Southern hospitality hangs. The Southern cafés and diners featured in the ***Dive Guide*** have dining rooms filled with customers, and many times lines out the door of faithful regulars who want a taste of home. In this book you will find the simplest to the most elaborate of biscuit recipes along with the secrets of biscuit making success. If you've never made homemade biscuit, pick an easy recipe, make it for those you love – and see what happens!

Biscuit History

The Southern biscuit has made a long journey on the road to culinary popularity. The biscuit, like many things, was born out of necessity in the days of the old South. Plantation and homestead cooks blended flour with water to make a practical staple – a biscuit. The earliest biscuits were utilitarian, inherited from the old country. Very much like the European flat cracker or cookie, these flat tasteless biscuits had a long shelf life and could be carried in the pockets of field hands and soldiers, often referred to as "hard tack" during the Civil War. The English and French word "*biscuit*" originates from the Latin *bis* meaning twice and *coctus* meaning cooked because at one time European biscuits were cooked twice to give them longer storage life.

But the Southern cooks' need to breathe some life into these flat practical tidbits took on a life of its own. The desire grew to make one's biscuit rise, to make one's biscuit tastier, to make one's biscuit better and more memorable than thy neighbor's biscuit offering. Cooks would come to add salt, hog lard, sugar, and heavy cream to their biscuit recipes. The focus was not just the taste but the look of the biscuit. Many plantations had their own leavening agents made out of wood ash, also called potash, to make their biscuits ascend. Some opted to make "beaten biscuits," in which cooks would literally beat and fold the biscuit dough hundreds of times with a triangular mallet to incorporate air to make their biscuits rise. The wealthy had a machine called a "biscuit brake" where two to three cooks working together would push and fold the dough through two rolling pin like ringers operated by a manual crank. These beaten biscuits became a status symbol of the South and are still made today in certain Southern social circles. Southern Chef Martha Stamps still makes beaten biscuits with her daughter and considers beaten biscuits a Southern tradition and delicacy to be remembered. You can see beaten biscuits being made in ***The Rise of the Southern Biscuit*** documentary.

This triangular mallet was used to beat air into biscuit dough in the early days of the South. Many cooks would beat the dough on a large stone.

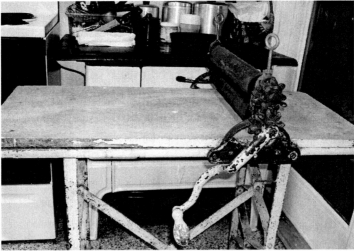

The well-to-do owned biscuit brakes in which the dough was cranked and folded through the two wringers. It took two to three cooks to get the job done.

So in the days of the Old South, the biscuit became the hallmark of the Southern homemaker and the standard offering to company. A biscuit stuffed with country ham became the symbol of Southern hospitality, and a guest always graciously accepted.

So, there you have it. The South is forever credited for putting the "rise" in the Southern biscuit – replacing the original lackluster practical flat biscuit with something feathery, light, and uniquely wonderful. That "unique" quality of the Southern biscuit has everything to do with the combination of ingredients you decide to use. Learn the basics and move forward with confidence as you enter the world of biscuit making.

Labels from Aunt Jane's popular beaten biscuits.

Biscuit Basics

A basic Southern biscuit is comprised of the following key ingredients: flour, fat, liquid, and a leavening agent. Learn about these ingredients, and take charge of your biscuit.

Flour Facts

Have you ever baked something from scratch, and it turned out like a brick? It is so baffling because you followed the recipe to the letter! Chances are the flour tripped you up. That's because there are different kinds of flour; the differences appear subtle, but they weigh in the outcome. To avoid biscuits that resemble hockey pucks, master the differences of flour, and master biscuit making.

Gluten

All flours contain gluten or protein, which is activated when you add liquid to flour and when you knead your dough. Every variety and brand of flour has different gluten levels, which impact the texture of your biscuit or any baked good.

Hard wheat flour has a high gluten content and is perfect for making elastic doughs that rise, like rolls, breads, and bagels - not good at all for the light Southern biscuit. Hard wheat has a 13% -15% gluten or protein content and is often labeled **bread flour.**

Soft wheat flour is perfect for biscuit making because it contains lower gluten levels which makes for a more airy outcome. Soft winter wheat has 4% - 9% gluten content.

Self -rising flour has baking powder and salt added to the flour and it has an 8 – 9% gluten content. Many biscuit makers whip up a three-ingredient biscuit using self rising flour, a fat, and a liquid. However, some bakers stay away from self-rising flour, because the baking powder can lose its zing if it's been on the shelf too long. It's a personal choice and has a lot to do with if you make biscuits often and know the flour is fresh.

All-purpose flour is a mixture of both soft and hard wheat flour with salt and baking powder added. Depending on the part of the country in which the flour is manufactured, you can have differing gluten content. Some have as high as a 12% gluten content. Southern flour companies offer all - purpose flour with an 8% gluten content, making it solely from soft wheat. **So if you're going to use all-purpose flour go with a Southern brand.**

Cake flour is made of soft wheat flour ground super fine, and it has low gluten content between 6 - 8%. It is also chlorinated to break down the gluten further to ensure a velvety smooth product. Some of our biscuit makers use cake flour.

Pastry flour is very similar to cake flour, only it is not chlorinated and has gluten content between 8 – 10 percent.

Flour Overview

For Southern biscuit making, use soft wheat flours,
preferably manufactured by a Southern flour company
because these products have a lower gluten content which
will give you a light biscuit. In this book, you'll be advised
over and over again by the biscuit makers, "Don't overwork
your dough." That's because the more you handle the dough,
the more activated the gluten becomes, and your biscuits will
turn out heavy instead of light and fluffy.

Rise, Biscuits, Rise!

The four ingredients you can use to make a baked good rise
are: yeast, baking powder, baking soda, and whipped egg
whites. Yeast and egg whites are rarely used because they
both take a lot of time. Biscuit making is traditionally fast
and easy. That's why baking powder and baking soda are the
preferred leavening agents for biscuit making.

Just like flours that seem similar yet are not, baking powder
and baking soda are very different, and you can ruin your
biscuits by thinking they're interchangeable. They are both
considered chemical agents and each reacts differently as you
"rise" your biscuits.

Baking Soda

A lot of the biscuit makers featured in this book love to use
baking soda in their biscuits. Baking soda is pure sodium
bicarbonate and produces gases when it comes into contact
with acid-based ingredients like buttermilk, sugar, or fruit
juices. An immediate reaction takes place as soon as the
soda and acidic ingredient are mixed the bowl. Time is

important here because the gases will dissipate if you wait too long to mix your biscuit dough, roll it, cut it, and get it into the oven. That's why many of our biscuit makers emphasize speed in biscuit making.

Baking Powder

Some of our biscuit makers prefer to use baking powder because it already contains the acidic element needed to leaven biscuits. Baking powder is a combination of baking soda (sodium bicarbonate) and the acidic salt, cream of tartar. Some brands add sodium aluminum sulphate or calcium acid phosphate, as well. The combination of these ingredients determines the two types of baking powder available to biscuit makers, which are single-acting baking powder and double-acting baking powder.

Single-Acting Baking Powder

When you use a "single-acting" baking powder, the rules of speed still apply to biscuit making. The chemical reaction, which produces gases to make your dough rise, takes place as soon as ingredients are mixed in the bowl. With "single acting" baking powder, you don't need an acidic ingredient like buttermilk because the baking powder already contains the acidic cream of tartar. So the benefit of a single acting baking powder is that you don't have to add an acidic element purposely to your recipe. You could make your biscuits with water, and they'd still rise to perfection.

Double-Acting Baking Powder

If you want to buy time and insurance, "double-acting" baking powder is the answer. It still has the immediate reaction in the mixing bowl like single action, but it also reacts a second time during the baking process. This is achieved by the addition of sodium aluminum sulphate, which reacts at high temperatures. Therefore, double-acting baking powder is activated during the mixing process and triggers a second time during the high temperature baking process.

Biscuit pitfalls

~ Avoid the temptation to add extra baking powder or baking soda to your biscuit recipe. Even though many of our biscuit makers do this, be careful because the extra bubbling action can cause your dough to rise so fast that the gas bubbles explode, which will leave you with a flat biscuit. Also, if you add too much baking powder, depending on the brand, it could add a bitter taste to your biscuits. Some of our biscuit makers avoid commercial baking powders for this reason. So adamant are they, that they make their own single acting baking powder by combining baking soda and cream of tartar.

~ If you're baking at a high altitude, use less baking soda or baking powder because carbon dioxide gas expands more quickly at high elevations.

~ How you choose to rise your biscuits is a personal choice having to do with taste and ease. Even though there are basic guidelines, many of our biscuit makers use combinations of leavening agents to get their biscuits a certain way.

~ One biscuit maker suggests adding whipped egg whites to ensure the leavening process. Southern Chef Miss Daisy King gives us her Angel Biscuit recipe which calls for yeast, baking powder, and baking soda – and the biscuits are not quick and easy, but wonderful! And the dough can keep in the refrigerator for days. Now that we know how to rise the biscuits, let's make them tasty.

Biscuit taste and texture

Biscuit Texture
Love your biscuit tender, love it flaky, or love it soft. Make your biscuit feel the way you want by realizing that your choice of fat will determine the texture of your biscuit. Be mindful that the more fat you add to your recipe the more crisp the biscuit, but too fat much will make it heavy. Less fat results in a soft biscuit.

Lard & Shortening
Both lard and shortening will produce a flaky biscuit. Lard will make the biscuit crisper; shortening will produce a more tender biscuit.

Butter & Margarine
Butter won't make your biscuit as flaky and tender as lard or shortening, but it adds great taste. Margarine will make a biscuit turn out softer than if you used butter, but it will be void of that buttery taste.

Alternative fats
Many biscuit makers combine fats to get the texture and taste they want.   One biscuit maker combines bacon fat with lard, others combine shortening or lard with butter to get the best of both worlds. A lot of our biscuit makers use one fat (butter) in the recipe and then brush the pan or the tops of the

biscuits with a different fat (lard) to get the combination they want.

Other fats that can be used in biscuits are peanut butter, mayonnaise, fat from wild game, and ground up country ham renderings.

I'm Melting
The colder the better when it comes to the fat you add to your biscuit dough. Don't allow lard, shortening, butter, or any fat to get warm and melt before you get your biscuits in the oven. Some biscuit makers are sticklers about this—others more lax. But if the fat softens, you'll have a flatter biscuit. Some biscuit makers insist on using cold butter or lard (one chef even freezes his lard) to make sure it's still in chunks at the rolling out stage. The chunks, or bits of fat, add volume to the uncooked biscuit and it just goes up from there when baked in the oven.

Liquid
The liquid used in a biscuit recipe definitely affects the taste and influences the texture. Buttermilk is an overwhelmingly popular choice, because of its taste and acidity which works well with baking soda as a leavening agent. However, any liquid can be used as long as the leavening aspect of the recipe is covered. From water to beer, soda pop, milk, heavy cream, orange juice, or skim milk, anything goes. This is where biscuit makers can get creative.

Restaurants

and

Recipes

*Outside of Mother's in New Orleans: On busy days, lines
form outside the doors of Mother's - a perfect chance to look
at the biscuit maker at work in the front window.*

The Biscuit Maker from The Old Mill in Pigeon Forge, Tennessee.

Alabama

Scoot over apple pie, it is biscuits that reign supreme in Alabama's baseball world. We have to give a shout out to the AA team owners who in 2003 made a bold move to bring the love of baseball and biscuits together—naming Alabama's team the "**Montgomery Biscuits**." The team's logo, "Monty," is a biscuit baseball loving character who must be a smooth talker because his tongue is a pat of butter. And yes, biscuits and honey sell like hotcakes at every home game. And the team's theme song is "Bring on the Biscuits."

Mobile

Tiny Diny
2159 Halls Mill Road
Mobile, Alabama
Hours: 5 a.m.-8 p.m Mon.-Fri. 5 a.m.-2 p.m. Sat.
(251) 473-9453
Biscuits served until they're gone

The Tiny Diny started out as just that in the 1950's – a tiny size diner on Halls Mill Road in Mobile, Alabama. Locals have eaten decades of homemade biscuits, breakfasts, and meat and three lunches at the "tiny dynasty." This is no ordinary diner – fresh fried oysters and catfish are among the 25 entrees offered on the menu. Everything here is homemade, like the award wining pancakes and syrup-like peach preserves.

Today, the Tiny Diny is located across the street from its original space, providing more elbow room to butter those homemade biscuits. The cooks at the Tiny Diny are up in their 80's and will not give out any of their recipes. Gail Silvester is part owner, and she says The Tiny Diny biscuits are absolutely "perfect." Here's her advice for best biscuit making.

Biscuit Advice: Gail says, "Don't use anything instant or fast in your biscuits." She's alluding to self-rising flour and all-purpose flour. Gail says, "Make your biscuits totally from scratch, no shortcuts. Gail is also a stickler for using Fleishmann's baking powder.

Georgia

Athens

Hoyt House Restaurant
295 E. Dougherty Street
Athens, GA 30601
Breakfast Daily 7:00 a.m. – 11:00 a.m.
(706) 549-7020
Biscuits served all hours

History and biscuits are the winning combination as you dine for breakfast at the historic Hoyt House in Athens, Georgia. Buttery biscuits with a citrus flavor are the standard offering of the day. Biscuits are served along side upscale Southern influenced cuisine in the opulently furnished surroundings.

At the Hoyt House, biscuits are served in three cozy dining rooms dotted with tables dressed in white linen. Six fireplaces add to the warm atmosphere of the restored two-story Nathan Hoyt home, which dates back to 1829.

The restaurant is part of The Foundry Park Inn Spa, a historic retreat which offers lodging and spa services. All diners are welcome at the Hoyt House and reservations are accepted.

Hoyt House Executive Chef Bret Clack believes Southern biscuits should live on a Southern menu. Chef Bret puts his own sweet twist on the classic Southern biscuit.

Hoyt House Biscuits

2 cups all-purpose flour
2 ounces of sugar
2 ounces of baking powder
1 ounce of honey
1 teaspoon orange zest
1 teaspoon baking soda
1 pound semi-soft butter
3 cups buttermilk

Preheat oven to 300F

Scale all ingredients; then sift dry ingredients together.

Fold the wet ingredients into the dry to make moist dough.

Knead the dough until firm; be careful not to over knead.

Divide dough in half and roll into ½ inch thick sheets and cut with a round cutter.

Place biscuits on greased sheet pan and bake at 300F for 15 minutes.

Atlanta

The Beautiful
2260 Cascade Road SW
Atlanta, Georgia 30331
Hours: Sunday-Thursday 7 a.m. – 11 p.m.
Friday and Saturday 24 hours
(404) 752-5931
Biscuits served for breakfast

Early in the morning you'll find Mother Mildred, The Beautiful's biscuit maker, effortlessly rolling out large batches of her homemade buttermilk biscuits. "Love," she says, is the most important ingredient that she puts in her biscuits, and The Beautiful customers love to eat them up. Mother Mildred and her beautiful biscuits were featured in ***The Rise of the Southern Biscuit*** documentary.

The Beautiful is an institution in Atlanta's African American community. Satisfying soul food is served "cafeteria style" seven-days a week. Breakfast on the line includes biscuits with African sausage, gravy, fried catfish, grits, eggs, and pancakes.

The Beautiful is owned and operated by members of the Perfect Church, which opened the restaurant in the 1979 as a way to employ its flock. Dishing up ribs and banana pudding, the smiling church ladies definitely add to the welcoming atmosphere. Celebrity sightings are routine, as actors, sports stars, and politicians come to The Beautiful to feed their souls.

Mother Mildred graciously shares The Beautiful's biscuit recipe. Remember, biscuits are only served for breakfast, and they go fast.

Biscuit Advice: Mother Mildred adds baking powder to the self-rising flour to get her beautiful biscuits just right. She says, "Make sure you add the baking powder to flour before adding anything else or the biscuits will not rise."

Beautiful Biscuits

1 bag all-purpose flour
1/2 cup of baking powder
3/4 cups shortening
½ gallon buttermilk

Preheat oven to 400F

Mix all-purpose flour with baking powder. Add shortening and mix with hands until you have pea-sized bits of flour.

Add buttermilk and mix into dough. Turn dough out onto a lightly floured surface and knead three to four times.

Roll dough out to a ½ inch thickness and place on ungreased baking pan. Bake at 400 for 10 to 15 minutes.

Behind the line at The Beautiful are the church ladies who dish up beautiful biscuits and gravy to faithful customers.

The Flying Biscuit Café (Midtown)
1001 Piedmont Avenue
Atlanta, GA 30309
Hours: Sun. – Thur. 7 a.m. – 10 p.m.
Fri. & Sat.7 a.m. –10:30 p.m.
(404) 874-8887
Biscuits served all day

For the "fairest" of them all try the tall gorgeous biscuits at the Flying Biscuit Café – a funky, cool, colorful place to dine. Often referred to as "The Biscuit" by regulars, diners enjoy the Southern style food that's been updated to include vegan and vegetarian offerings.

The Flying Biscuit serves breakfast all day and routinely wins the "Best of Atlanta" award for favorite biscuit. This colorful fun biscuit eatery is a Southern biscuit must. Breakfast, lunch, or dinner, no matter, every guest gets the "gift" of a biscuit—a genuine gesture of Southern hospitality. And the vegan gravy on a flying biscuit? Out of this world!

Flying Biscuit chef and owner, Delia Champion has worked years to perfect her biscuit recipe. You can watch her make her Flying biscuits in the documentary, ***The Rise of the Southern Biscuit.***

Delia estimates that about seven-thousand biscuits are served at her two restaurants every week. To accommodate all tastes, a whole wheat "Flying Biscuit" is offered, as well. The signature biscuits are served with homemade cranberry-apple butter, which is always simmering on the stove; they also are served along side egg dishes and offered as grand breakfast sandwiches too.

Biscuit making is Delia's passion. She is more than happy to share her "Flying Biscuit" recipe and biscuit making tips.

Biscuit Advice: Delia says, "Never, never overwork the dough. Knead it four times and stop. If you handle the dough too much, you won't have tall, wonderful biscuits."

Delia uses light cream in her biscuits which is hard to find at grocery stores. It has an 18 percent fat content. So the combination of heavy cream and half and half is substituted below.

The Flying Biscuit

3 cups all-purpose flour
1 tablespoon plus 1 ½ teaspoons baking powder
¾ teaspoon salt
3 tablespoons plus 1 ½ teaspoons sugar
6 tablespoons unsalted butter at room temperature
2/3 cup heavy cream
2/3 cup half and half

Preheat oven to 350F, and line a sheet pan with parchment paper.

Place flour, baking powder, salt, and sugar in a large mixing bowl. Cut butter into ½ tablespoon-sized bits and add to the flour. Using your hands, work the butter into the dry ingredients. Mix until butter is cut into the size of small peas.

Make a well in the center of the flour and pour in all the heavy cream and ½ cup half and half.

Stir the dry ingredients into the wet by using your hand in a circular fashion to knock the flour into the liquid. Stir just enough until the dough comes together into a sticky ball. Turn dough onto a lightly floured surface, and knead four times.

Using a lightly-floured rolling pin, roll the dough into a 1-inch thickness. The correct thickness is the key to making your biscuits fly.

Dip a 2 ½ inch biscuit cutter in flour; then cut the dough. Repeat until all of the dough has been cut. Scraps can be gathered together and re-rolled one more time.

Place the biscuits on the prepared sheet pan, leaving about ¼ inch between them.

Brush the tops of the biscuits with 1 tablespoon of half and half, and sprinkle with 1 tablespoon of sugar.

Bake for 20 to 23 minutes. Biscuits will be lightly browned on top and flaky in the center when done.

Makes 8 – 12 biscuits depending on the size of the cutter.

The Flying Biscuit's second location is 1655 McClendon Avenue in Candler Park, (404) 678-8888

Delia says her Flying Biscuit recipe evolved as she and her bakers worked at making a biscuit that their customers would love. She says "TALL" was overwhelmingly popular. So there you have it.

Mammy's

968 Memorial Drive SE
Atlanta, Georgia 30316
Hours: breakfast and lunch Mon. – Fri. 6 a.m. – 1:30 p.m.
breakfast only Sunday 6 a.m. – 12:30 p.m.
(404) 525-9110
Biscuits served all day

Generations of Atlantans along with politicians and civil rights leaders have frequented this cozy, country-style diner, located just two miles from the State Capitol.

For more than 30 years, Mammy's has served breakfast all day including hot biscuits with country ham. Mammy's homemade biscuits and fresh meat slicing policy makes this a Southern dining must. Mammy's owner Barry Stangline says, "It just tastes better when each order of country ham, pork chops, and smoked ham is sliced fresh to order before cooking."

Mammy's biscuit recipe is a well guarded secret. Barry does advise that when it comes to Southern cooking, make it from scratch and with the best ingredients and you can't go wrong.

Thumbs Up

573 Edgewood Avenue SE
Atlanta, GA 30312
Hours: Breakfast & Lunch Mon- Fri. 7 a.m. – 3 p.m.
Saturday and Sunday 8 a.m. – 4 p.m.
(404) 223-0690
Biscuits served all hours

Thumbs Up continues to get the urban "thumbs up" from faithful breakfast goers who literally eat up the tall multi-grain biscuits concocted by owner and biscuit maker, Lou Lockicchio. Lou makes his biscuits to suit his personal taste, and he's gone through a lot of trouble to make that happen.

Lou's biscuits, one-pan potato and egg dishes, and fabulous French toast are mainstays of the diner. The brick walls and burgundy booths make this a warm and inviting place to eat breakfast.

Lou's been making his biscuits for more than 20 years and recently opted to contract a mill to blend his flour for him. Get this, Lou even makes his own baking powder, which he says doesn't have the "distasteful" aluminum flavor of most commercial baking powders.

Lou mixes his biscuit flour in large batches; so below, he shares the ingredients he uses to make his popular multi-grain biscuits.

Biscuit Advice: Lou says mix white self-rising flour, whole wheat flour, rye flour, and oats to make his multi-grain blend.

Lou also recommends European margarine, which is a blend of butter and margarine. Like his homemade baking powder, Lou says the European margarine has a superior taste.

Conyers

Mammie's Kitchen Biscuits
1294 North Main Street
Conyers, GA 30012
Hours: Mon. – Sat 5 a.m. – 2 p.m.
Breakfast all day
(770) 922-0131
Biscuits served all hours

When it comes to biscuit making, Mammie's biscuit-making technique is the epitome of the saying "time and trouble." The small, no-frills breakfast haunt hinges its reputation on its labor intensive, handmade biscuits that are served to diners. Mammie's biscuit maker, Miss Pat Morgan, hand rolls each individual biscuit. No biscuit cutters allowed! Talk about dedication, but oh so worth it.

Along with the usual bacon and sausage biscuit, Mammies Kitchen Biscuits is known for its Strick-o-lean biscuit. Strick-o-lean is a thick, wide cut of bacon with a rind that's sliced fresh to order and then fried crisp and stuffed into one of Pat's handmade biscuits. It's a number one seller. Breakfast is served all day with daily country-style lunch specials. Order at the counter or wheel through the drive-thru.

Miss Pat says Mammie's biscuits are "blessed" because she prays every day before work and even while she's making the biscuits. Miss Pat says her biscuits turn out pretty and fluffy. Here's the recipe.

Mammie's Kitchen Biscuits Recipe

1 bag of all-purpose flour
1 handful of lard
½ gallon of buttermilk with a little extra to make dough wet

Preheat oven to 400F.

Mix lard into the flour using your hands until the mixture resembles course cornmeal. Add buttermilk and use a little extra than you normally think you'd need. Mix the dough and leave it in bowl.

Dust your hands with flour and pull of pieces of dough and hand roll them. Place them on a pan and, using your palm, mash them down flat. Bake in oven at 400 for 10 to 15 minutes.

Dalton

Mr. Biscuit
1904 Chattanooga Road
Dalton, Georgia
Hours: 6a.m.–2 p.m. – Mon.—Sat.
(706) 226-4314
Biscuits served all hours

On most days, you'll find Pauline Brown taking orders and working the cash register at his home away from home, Mr. Biscuit. Since he was 14 years old, Pauline has worked at the restaurant his aunt and uncle opened in Dalton, Georgia in the 1970's. Making biscuits, a lifetime of them, is part of Pauline's heritage as the "Mr. Biscuit" biscuit recipe is his mother's.

Mr. Biscuit is a little, old-fashioned, country café known for its biscuits, country ham, and down-home cooking. Breakfast is offered all day, and nothing but from-scratch southern cooking, like chicken and dumplings and fried chicken, comes out of the kitchen.

However, the biscuits here are king! Pauline says his famous biscuits are white and fluffy because he uses milk instead of buttermilk. Here's the recipe and Pauline's biscuit tip.

Biscuit Advice: Pauline recommends using whole milk in your biscuit recipe. He believes buttermilk turns biscuits yellow and makes them hard. He says whole milk keeps his biscuits bright white and soft on the insides.

Mr. Biscuit Biscuit Recipe

1 bag of all-purpose flour
2 handfuls of shortening
½ gallon milk
quart of water

Preheat oven to 400F

Using your hands, mix two handfuls of shortening into flour. Add milk and water combine until dough forms. Turn the dough out onto a floured surface and flip it three times. Roll out and cut. Bake for 10 to 15 minutes at 400F.

Decatur

Crescent Moon
174 West Ponce de Leon Avenue
Decatur, GA
Hours: Tue. – Fri.7:30 a.m. – 9:30 p.m.
Saturday 7:30 a.m. – 3p.m. dinner 5:30 – 9:30 p.m.
Sunday & Monday 7:30 a.m. – 3 p.m.
(404) 377-5623
Biscuits served all hours

Non-stop breakfast is the draw at the Crescent Moon, a funky retro diner that's proclaimed as downtown Decatur's best biscuit and breakfast bet. The fresh baked, oh-so-high, multi-grain biscuits are served with eggs, grits, and sausage. The 4-inch wonders also come with country ham, pork sausage, and chicken sausage. The Crescent Moon dishes up your typical diner fare for lunch and dinner.

Crescent Moon's biscuit maker, Rob Atherholt, hand mixes the large batches of multi-grain flour together and adds a touch of sour cream to create his original biscuits.

Rob says his biscuits come out of the oven, just slightly darker than a white flour biscuit. Here's how he does it.

Biscuit Advice: Rob says when mixing multi-grains keep it to a six to one ratio. This means to use mostly white flour and keep other alternative grain flour to a lesser amount. For example, if you add too much oat or wheat flour, you'll get a heavy biscuit that won't rise.

Crescent Moon Multi-grain Biscuits

6 cups self-rising white flour
½ cup wheat flour
½ cup oat flour
1 cup of oats
½ teaspoon salt
½ cup shortening
¼ cup sour cream
1 ½ cups buttermilk (add just enough to make the mixture moist)

Preheat oven to 400F.

In a bowl, combine the flours and oats; then add salt. Cut in shortening until the mixture resembles cornmeal. Add sour cream and buttermilk. Remember to add the buttermilk slowly and add just enough to make the mixture moist.

Lightly flour your work surface and roll the dough out to 1 ½ inch thickness. This thickness will make a tall biscuit. Bake in 400 degree oven for 20 minutes.

Pastries A-Go-Go
235 Ponce de Leon Place
Decatur, GA 30030
Hours: breakfast 7:30 a.m. – 2:30 p.m. Mon.Wed.Thur.Fri.
Bakery 7:30 a.m – 4:00 p.m. Mon.Wed.Thur.Fri.
Brunch 7:30 a.m. – 2:30 p.m. Saturday & Sunday
Closed Tuesdays
(404) 373-3423
Biscuits Served All Hours

Authentic Southern "cathead" biscuits are all the rave at Pastries A-Go-Go in Decatur, Georgia. You always hear old-timers in the South talk about cathead biscuits. These biscuits are? You guessed it. As big as a cat's head. The local paper names Pastries A-Go-Go's catheads as Decatur's "best" biscuit. Breakfast and biscuits are served all hours at this popular bakery/café. You can dine in or order something to-go-go from the yummy filled bakery case.

Owner Bob Light came up with his cathead biscuit recipe ten years ago. He says good biscuit making takes practice and more practice to develop the right technique.

Biscuit Advice: Flour dough very lightly on top to keep the inside wet while rolling out.

Pastry A-Go-Go Cathead Biscuits

3 pounds cake flour
½ ounce salt
2 ounces baking powder
2 ounces granulated sugar
1 pound of butter, softened
1 quart buttermilk

Preheat oven to 375F.

In electric mixing bowl combine all dry ingredients together.

Add butter and mix at low speed for 30 seconds then add buttermilk, incorporate well. This will form wet dough.

Bob Light's catheads!

Turn dough out onto a floured surface, roll out and cut with large biscuit cutter (3 ½ - 4 inch) to achieve "cathead" size.

Brush tops of baked biscuits with butter.

Watershed

406 West Ponce de Leon Avenue
Decatur, GA 30030
Hours: Lunch & Dinner Mon.–Sat. 11a.m. – 10 p.m.
Sunday Brunch 10 a.m. – 3 p.m.
(404) 378-4900
Biscuits served Sunday brunch and Tuesday nights

Awards, accolades, and rave reviews define Watershed's sterling Southern culinary reputation. It's an upscale dining experience with down-home Southern flavor. Daily specials are on the menu, with Executive Chef Scott Peacock's award winning fried chicken served every Tuesday night—as are his lard-buttermilk and vegetarian cream biscuits.

Chef Peacock's mentor and biscuit advisor was Edna Lewis, an African-American chef and cookbook author –a deemed expert on Southern cooking. The Watershed biscuits are pricked on top, somewhat like a beaten biscuit, giving them an old fashioned look.

Biscuits are also served at the Southern Sunday Brunch with favorites like country ham with red eye gravy.

Chef Peacock is a biscuit stickler. He even makes his own baking powder. He shares his biscuit and baking powder recipes from *The Gift of Southern Cooking*, by Edna Lewis and Scott Peacock.

Biscuit Advice: Chef Peacock says, "Learn how to work your dough to the right consistency. If the dough is too wet your biscuits will be heavy. If the dough is dry your biscuits will crumble." Scott suggests kneading biscuit dough about 8 to 10 times.

Bake your biscuits at a high temperature to achieve the duality of a crunchy exterior and a soft inside.

Make your own baking powder to avoid the metallic taste and preservatives in commercial baking powder.

Don't re-roll your dough after first biscuit cutting. Don't twist the biscuit cutter, go up and down.

Watershed's Buttermilk Biscuits

5 cups sifted flour (measured after sifting)
1 tablespoon plus ½ teaspoon homemade baking powder
1 tablespoon kosher salt
½ cup packed lard, chilled
1 ¼ cups buttermilk
3 tablespoons unsalted butter, melted. (to brush on top)

Preheat oven to 500F.

Put the flour, homemade baking powder, and salt in a mixing bowl, and whisk well to blend thoroughly.

Add the lard, and working quickly, coat it in the flour and rub between your fingers until approximately half the lard is finely blended and the other half remains in large pieces, about ½ inch in size.

Pour in the buttermilk, and stir quickly, just until the dough is blended, and begins to mass.

Turn the dough immediately out onto a floured surface, and with floured hands knead briskly eight to ten times, until the dough becomes cohesive.

Gently flatten the dough with your hands into a disk of even thinness. Then using a floured rolling pin, roll it out to a uniform thickness of ½ inch. With a dinner fork dipped in flour, pierce completely through the dough at half-inch intervals.

Lightly flour a 2 ½ or 3-inch biscuit cutter, and stamp out rounds. Do not twist the cutter in the dough. Cut the biscuits from the dough as close together as you can for maximum yield. Transfer biscuits to a parchment lined baking sheet, placing them so they just barely kiss. Don't re-roll the scraps. Just arrange them around the edge of the sheet and bake them as "cook's treat."

Put the baking sheet immediately on the center rack of the preheated oven. Bake 10-12 minutes, checking after six minutes or so, turning the pan in needed for even baking. When the biscuits are golden brown, remove from oven, and brush the tops with melted butter.

Watershed's Baking Powder

Cream of tartar
Baking Soda

Mix two parts cream of tartar with one part baking soda. Store in an airtight container away from light. It will have a shelf life of two weeks.

Savannah

The Lady & Sons
102 West Congress St.
Savannah, GA 31401
Hours: Lunch Monday - Saturday 11a.m. – 3 p.m.
Dinner Monday – Saturday begins at 5 p.m.
Sunday Buffet 11a.m. – 5p.m.
(912) 233-2600
Biscuits served all day

It's all in the family, a very Southern family, when it comes to The Lady & Sons, restaurant in Georgia. Eager diners line up out the door and into the Savannah street waiting to get a taste of celebrity chef Paula Dean's authentic Southern cooking.

Dean's signature cheese biscuits brushed with garlic butter are prepared by the thousands at The Lady & Sons. Biscuits are a mainstay of a' la carte menu and the sumptuous Southern lunch and dinner buffets offered daily.

Diners love the simple, high-quality, Southern cooking that has brought Paula Dean to fame. Paula owns and operates her famed restaurant with her two sons, Jamie and Bobby – and her biscuits are legendary.

Paula Dean's Garlic Cheese Biscuits

1 ¼ cups of biscuit mix (Paula Dean sells her own or use your own biscuit recipe flour mixture and add the following)
½ cup grated sharp cheddar cheese
½ cup of water

Garlic Butter
½ stick unsalted butter, melted
¼ teaspoon garlic powder
¼ teaspoon salt
1/8 teaspoon dried parsley flakes

Preheat the oven to 400 degrees, and line a baking sheet with parchment paper.

Combine the biscuit mix and cheese in a small bowl. Add the water and stir just until combined. The dough will be slightly moist. Drop spoonfuls of dough onto the prepared baking sheet. Bake for about 10 minutes until the biscuits are firm and begin to brown.

While the biscuits are baking, prepare the garlic butter by combining the butter, garlic powder, salt, and parsley flakes in a small bowl. Mix well. As soon as you bring the biscuits from the oven, brush them with the garlic butter using a pastry brush.

Mrs. Wilkes Dining Room
107 West Jones Street
Savannah, GA 31401
Hours: Family Style Lunch Mon. – Fri. 11a.m. – 2 p.m.
(912) 232-5997
Biscuits served all hours

Sema Wilkes is lovingly remembered in Savannah Georgia, where her good name is synonymous with excellent family-style Southern cooking. Mrs. Wilkes owned and operated her boarding house in Savannah for years until the boarding house slowly evolved into a restaurant as she allowed outsiders to join her residents for dinner.

Sema's hospitality and dependable recipes are carried on as her children operate Mrs. Wilkes Dining Room. Diners from all over come to eat family-style at what they call, "The Old Boarding House"or "Mrs. Wilkes." The fabulous comfort food is often written up in newspapers and magazines as a Southern favorite.

Mrs. Wilkes' biscuits are not made with a biscuit cutter but hand rolled; no two look alike. Lunch is served family style with combinations of guests seated together at large dining tables. Five main dishes and up to 17 vegetables and sides are passed, yes, to the left, and so are the biscuits.

Mrs. Wilkes' biscuit recipe is detailed. Follow it, and make wonderful biscuits.

Biscuit Advice: Mrs. Wilkes combined buttermilk, whole milk, and water to make her dough instead of a single liquid. She also combined Crisco and butter instead of using one fat in her biscuit recipe.

Mrs. Wilkes Biscuits

2 cups self-rising
½ teaspoon baking powder
1 teaspoon Crisco
2 tablespoons of margarine or butter
1/3 cup buttermilk
1/3 cup whole milk
water

Preheat oven to 450F.

Sift flour and baking powder together in a bowl. Cut butter and Crisco into the flour.

Fill a measuring cup with combination of buttermilk, whole milk and water. Make a well in the middle your flour mixture and pour ¾ cup of the liquid in and mix lightly and quickly to form dough moist enough to leave sides of bowl.

Turn dough onto a lightly floured surface and coat your hands with flour. Knead six times by picking the dough up by the sides and pushing it away from you with palms down. Pinch off pieces of dough and form balls; press flat to shape and place on a well greased pan. Bake in a 450 degree oven for 12 to 15 minutes.

Kentucky

Belfry

Tudor's Biscuit World

26375 US Highway 119 N
Belfry, Kentucky
Hours: Daily 4:30 a.m. – 10 p.m.
(606) 353-8899
Biscuits served all hours

Here's a chain restaurant that's gone through the trouble to keep it "homemade." Tudor's Biscuit World in Belfry serves made-from-scratch, Southern biscuits from over the counter and through the drive-thru. Biscuits are served all day long and many old timers come to Tudor's to eat biscuits, drink coffee, and hang out.

This little place is located in a gas station. Folks on the run can get breakfast till two in the afternoon and Southern home cooking to go after 10 a.m. Bill Tudor founded the restaurant in the 1980's and his biscuit recipe is kept hush hush!

There are 50 Tudor's Biscuit Worlds located mostly in Virginia and West Virginia. So if you see a Tudor's and crave a biscuit, wheel on in!

Glasgow

More Comfort Food Southern Restaurant
1201 West Main Street
Glasgow, KY 42411
Hours: breakfast & lunch 5:15 a.m. – 5 p.m.
(270) 651-8537
Biscuits served all hours

The name of this restaurant sums up the foreseen eating adventure. Tasty, down-home, cooking is served at The More Comfort Food Southern Restaurant. Homemade biscuits, fried pies, fried chicken, and slow-simmered pinto beans are just a few of the comfort foods served on the line at this Glasgow favorite.

The abundance of daily selections are served hot and fresh, cafeteria style. There's nothing fancy here, just uncomplicated goodness.

Biscuit maker Mildred Shaw is in charge of keeping a steady stream of fresh biscuits coming out of the oven and onto the line. She says customers comment on how the biscuits look different every day. She says that's how you know they're homemade!

If you don't like involved recipes, you'll love Mildred's popular, no fuss biscuit winner.

Biscuit Advice: Make biscuits fast and bake them even faster in a 500F oven.

More Southern Comfort Food Biscuits

2 cups of all-purpose flour
½ cup shortening
½ cup milk

Preheat oven to 500F

Put flour in a bowl, and cut in shortening. Add milk and blend to form dough. On a lightly floured surface, knead the dough a few times, and roll it out with a lightly floured rolling pin.

Cut biscuits, and place on a cookie sheet.

Bake a 500F until golden brown.

Louisville

Lilly's
1147 Bardstown Road
Louisville, Kentucky 40204
Hours: lunch Tue.-Sat 11 a.m. – 3:00 p.m.
Dinner Tue—Sat. 5:30 p.m.–10 p.m
Dinner Fri. & Sat.5:30 p.m. – 11 p.m.
(502) 451-0447
Biscuits served for dinner only

Celebrated Chef Kathy Carry brings Southern cooking to a new level at her popular restaurant, Lilly's in Louisville, Kentucky. Kathy serves her lovely biscuits in a variety of creative dishes, infusing Southern tradition with taste.

Cathy serves her flaky homemade Southern biscuits with venison, Kentucky ham, as the centerpiece for her escargot, and with pan seared fois gras, drizzled with cider reduction.

Lilly's is a colorful, peaceful place to dine and the menu changes as fresh ingredients come into season. A customer favorite is Kathy's pot pie, which graced the cover of *Bon Appetit.*

Kathy shares her recipe for biscuit success.

Biscuit Advice: Kathy says, "Make your biscuits fast. Don't fiddle with the dough. Get the biscuits into the oven quickly. Use chilled butter, and leave chunks in the dough to make the biscuit flaky."

Kathy Carry's Southern Biscuits

2 cups flour
2 teaspoons baking powder
½ teaspoon baking soda
1 teaspoon salt
¼ pound chilled butter chopped very fine
1 cup buttermilk

Preheat oven to 425F.

Line a baking pan with parchment paper.

Using a food processor combine flour with chopped chilled butter, and pulse quickly to mix. Only pulse a few times.

Transfer mixture to a bowl, and quickly add buttermilk.

Using hands mix the dough.

On a lightly floured surface, turn dough once and pat out. Cut biscuits and place on parchment papered pan. Put them in the oven immediately, and bake for 8 – 12 minutes.

Limestone Restaurant
10001 Forest Green Blvd.
Louisville, KY 40223
Hours: lunch Mon. – Fri. 11 a.m. – 2 p.m.
Dinner Mon. – Thu. 5 p.m.–10 p.m.
Weekend Hours Fri. & Sat. 5 p.m. – 10:30 p.m.
(502) 426-7477
Biscuits served as dessert and special dishes

Kentucky Bourbon and all its goodness is celebrated at the Limestone Restaurant in Louisville, Kentucky. Chefs Jim Gerhardt and Michael Cunha hold their bourbon and Southern biscuits close to their culinary hearts. The main ingredient in the pair's Sour Mash Biscuit recipe is the mash from distilled bourbon.

The two define their cuisine as "New Southern Cooking" served with old "Southern Charm".

Chef Gerhardt says the mash gives his biscuits a "nutty" flavor. The sour mash biscuits are served with fois gras as an appetizer and as a dessert smothered with bourbon-marinated berries.

Other items on the menu include braised beef short ribs with smoky white beans and fried green tomatoes with roasted garlic aioli. The Southern infused menu is offered with a world class bourbon selection and international wine list.

The Limestone has their own blend of mash and winter wheat flour milled for them. This biscuit mixture is wet, so they actually spoon out the dough and roll it in flour before dropping it onto the baking pan.

Limestone Sour Mash Drop Biscuits

2   cups of sour mash and flour mix
1 cup milk

Preheat oven to 450F

Pour the milk into the mash flour mix, and let it stand to absorb the liquid.   The mixture will be very wet.

In another bowl pour additional flour mixture. Spoon out wet mixture, and roll in dry flour. Place on a well greased cookie sheet. Bake in a 450F oven for 15-20 minutes, and brush with melted butter when they come out of the oven.

Lynn's Paradise Café
984 Barret Avenue
Louisville, KY 40204
Hours Mon. – Fri. 7 a.m. –10 p.m.
Saturday & Sunday 8 a.m. –10 p.m.
(502) 583-3447

If you want to have a blast and eat some of the best Southern biscuits ever, take a trip to Lynn's Paradise Café in Louisville, Kentucky. Breakfast and full menu are served all hours. Lynn Winter and her wildly wonderful restaurant,

49

staff, and famous biscuits are featured in the documentary, *The Rise of the Southern Biscuit.*

As soon as you arrive at Lynn's Paradise, from the parking lot to the restrooms, you'll find fun wacky art that will make you smile. Twinkle lights, trees, and whimsical lamps decorate this Southern café which serves crusty, square, tall, big biscuits.

Lynn Winter is the mastermind behind the café who, under the tutelage of two of her Southern cooking mentors, came up with the giant drop biscuit recipe that has put her on the Southern biscuit making map.

After Lynn mixes the dough, she drops it onto a giant cookie sheet, spreads it out, brushes it with butter, precuts the raw dough into square biscuits, and bakes them. This eliminates the "rolling out" step, she says. The precutting provides perforated squares that can be easily dished up. Here's Lynn's Paradise recipe.

Biscuit Advice: Brush the tops of unbaked biscuits with real butter, not margarine. In fact, always use real butter in any aspect of biscuit making. This dough is extremely sticky. Resist the urge to add more flour, and don't overwork or touch the dough too much; that leads to a flat biscuit.

Lynn's Paradise Biscuits

4   cups flour
4 teaspoons baking powder
1 ¼ teaspoons salt
1 teaspoon baking soda
2/3 cup solid vegetable shortening
1 ½ cups buttermilk
1 cup heavy cream
2 tablespoons butter –melted

Preheat over to 425F.

In a large bowl, sift together the flour, baking powder, salt, and baking soda.

Cut the shortening into the flour mixture with a pastry blender until the shortening is the size of small peas.

Pour in the buttermilk and cream. Fold and blend together with a rubber spatula. The dough will be sticky and wet.

Prepare a 9 x 9, 2-inch baking pan with non-stick spray. Spoon the batter into the pan, and even it out with the rubber spatula. Dust your hands with flour, and lightly pat the dough until it is even and is pressed into the corners of the pan.
Using a floured table knife or pastry cutter, cut through the dough to make 16-square biscuits. Brush with melted butter, and bake for 30 –35 minutes. Test to make sure the biscuits are done by carefully lifting the crust of the middle biscuit and poking the biscuit underneath. The biscuit should spring back when pressed. If the dough still seems wet and spongy,

put the biscuits back in the oven for an additional five minutes or until firm.

Remove the biscuits from the oven, and allow them to rest for five minutes before cutting. Serve with butter, sorghum butter, or sausage gravy.

Lynn Winter's whimsical personality is reflected in the tall buttery Southern biscuits she loves to serve. Her macaroni and cheese was also featured on Oprah.

Sulphur Well

The Lighthouse Restaurant
1500 Sulphur Well Knob Lick Road (Hwy. 70)
Sulphur Well, Kentucky 42129
Hours: Tue. – Thu. 10 a.m. – 7 p.m.
Friday – Saturday 10 a.m. – 9 p.m.
(270) 565-3095
Biscuits served all hours

A country store and The Lighthouse Restaurant are the only two businesses that stand in Sulphur Well, Kentucky. This well known mom and pop restaurant is a worthwhile, out of the way, trip for many biscuit eaters.

The Lighthouse is routinely packed. Here you can get breakfast served all day and "all you can eat" family-style dinners featuring homemade biscuits.

The Lighthouse signature biscuits topped with red eye gravy are served with bottomless platters of country ham, fried chicken, and catfish. Homemade pies and coleslaw are also served in abundance to diners who waddle away.

Lighthouse biscuit maker Shirley Dowell turns her biscuits out tirelessly. She keeps it simple by using all-purpose flour, lard, and milk.

Lighthouse owner Rodney Decker says it's a tribute to his Southern biscuits and cooking that so many customers travel to his small town just to eat.

Louisiana

Baton Rouge

Frank's Restaurant and Smokehouse
8353 Airline Highway
Baton Rouge, Louisiana 70815-8114
Hours: Daily 5 a.m. – 2:30 p.m.
(225) 926-5977
Biscuits served all day

"If you can choke it we can smoke it!" No kidding, that's the motto at Frank's. This very popular smokehouse restaurant is famous for its smoked meats and more so for its cathead biscuits. It's really hard to know where to start when talking about biscuits and Frank's Smokehouse.

So popular is "Daddy" Frank's secret biscuit recipe that the restaurant offers "biscuit birthday cakes" for customers who call ahead. When you come to Frank's you can be choosy. If you prefer tall tender biscuit, order your biscuit from the middle of the pan, if crisp is what you like, order your biscuit from the edge of the pan.

The catheads are served with seven types of sausage, including boudin. They are topped with sausage gravy, creamed chicken, fruit and sugar, syrup, and barbecue brisket. One fourth of July, Frank's biscuit maker used food coloring to make the biscuits red, white, and blue. In the morning, local businesses order boxes of catheads to go. The biscuit mania goes on and on.

Service at Frank's is friendly. Most of the wait staff is related to one another in some form or fashion. Breakfast is served all day, and smoked brisket, chicken, turkey, pork loin, and ribs are just a few of the meats that are smoked at Frank's.

"Daddy" Frank's cathead biscuit recipe is off limits. We do know that an empty cranberry can is used as the biscuit cutter.

There's a second Frank's Smokehouse in Prairieville, Louisiana. (225) 673-8876.

Louie's Café
209 West State Street
Baton Rouge, Louisiana 70802
Hours: open 24 hours a day 7-days a week
(225) 346-8221
Biscuits served all day

Biscuits and breakfast are served 24/7 at Louie's Café located right off the north gate of the Louisiana State University Campus in Baton Rouge. Louie's has been serving biscuits since 1941, and the old fashioned diner bustles with non-stop business. Biscuits topped with homemade white and brown gravy are offered along with every type of breakfast food you can imagine.

Biscuits at Louie's are of the big and fluffy variety, the biscuit recipe is kept a secret. However, Fred Simonson has been Louie's main biscuit maker for 10 years and shares his biscuit making secrets.

Biscuit Advice: Unlike most biscuit recipes, do not add the buttermilk or liquid portion of your recipe to the flour. Do it just the opposite, Brad advises. When you add the flour to the liquid, you can control the consistency of your dough.

Brad does not use a rolling pin but his hands to pat the dough into a disc. He says rolling pins stretch and tear the top layer of the dough. He also cuts his biscuits ¾ inches thick, which makes for a really tall biscuit.

New Orleans –French Quarter

K-Paul's Louisiana Kitchen
416 Chartres Street
New Orleans, LA 70130
Hours: Dinner Mon. – Sat. 5:30 p.m. – 10 p.m.
Lunch Fri. & Sat. 11:30 a.m. to 2:30 p.m.
(504) 524-7394
Biscuits served all hours

In the heart of the French Quarter you'll find the beat of New Orleans finest cooking. Chef Paul Prudhomme's K-Paul's Louisiana Kitchen turns out incredible entrees laced with his fabulous spice combinations and tasty sauces. Chef Paul is often in the dining room making himself available to sign cookbooks and talk with culinary fans.

The food is upscale served with Southern hospitality. The dining room is cozy yet fashionable. The brick walls are accented by original artwork of Chef Paul's famous recipes.

The anticipated prelude to Chef Paul's meals is the breadbasket of black molasses muffins, cheese and jalapeno yeast rolls, plain yeast rolls, and his Southern biscuit muffins. The biscuit muffins have a slight crispy crunch on the edges.

Sarah Woods is K-Paul's head baker and biscuit maker. It's her job to keep the packed dining room supplied in biscuits, muffins, rolls, and desserts. Sarah's bakery is above the restaurant. She showed us how it's done.

Biscuit Advice: Sarah says keep the butter cold. For her the cold butter keeps the biscuit mixture at the right consistency for a successful muffin/biscuit.

Sarah Woods taking Paul Prudhomme's famous Southern biscuit muffins out of the oven.

K-Paul's Southern Biscuit Muffins

2 ½ cups all-purpose flour
¼ cup sugar
1 ½ tablespoons baking powder
¼ teaspoon salt
¼ pound (one stick) plus 2 tablespoons of unsalted butter
1 cup cold milk

Preheat oven to 350F.

In a bowl, combine the flour, sugar, baking powder and salt; mix well, breaking up any lumps. Work the butter in by hand until the mixture resembles coarse cornmeal, making sure no lumps are left. Gradually stir in the milk, mixing just until dry ingredients are moistened. Do not overbeat. Spoon the batter into 1 greased muffin cups. Bake at 350 degrees until golden brown, about 35 to 40 minutes. The finished muffins should have a thick crust with a cake-like center.

A close look at the crusty petite biscuit muffins served at K-Paul's.

Mother's Restaurant
401 Poydras Street
New Orleans, LA 70130
Hours: Sun. – Thu. 7 a.m – 8 p.m.
Fri. & Sat 9 a.m. – 10 p.m
(504) 523-9656
Biscuits served all hours

On the fringe of the French Quarter sits the famed Mother's Restaurant where biscuits topped with debris, black ham, baked ham, and fried ham are dished up all day long.

Sausage and cream gravy are nowhere to be found at Mother's - just "debris" - tender shavings of roast beef in au jus served in heaping amounts over fresh homemade biscuits. Biscuit lovers grapple with the decision to either go with debris or one of the smoked cured hams that's made Mother's so legendary.

The owners of Mother's claim that the term debris was coined decades ago when a customer asked the then owner who was carving roast beef, "Can I have a piece of that debris in the bottom of the pan?" Today debris is no accident as 50 gallon batches of debris are made up at a time to satisfy the demand for the beef topped biscuits.

Mother's serves about 500 biscuits a day and about one thousand biscuits on the weekends. It's added fun to watch the biscuit maker in the window from the street outside of Mother's.

Chef Proprietor Jerry Amato says that Mother's bakes at least 500 biscuits a day.

Mother' Debris Recipe

1 4-5 pound bottom round roast, untrimmed. Ask your butcher to leave some fat on for cooking purposes.
1 teaspoon salt
1 teaspoon ground black pepper
1 teaspoon granulated onion
1 teaspoon granulated garlic
1/2 teaspoon dried thyme
2 medium yellow onions, quartered
3 medium carrots, halved
3 celery ribs, halved
12 cups beef stock to cover meat (recipe to follow)
1 brown craft paper bag with no print to wrap around the roast.

Preheat oven to 350F.

Combine dry seasoning and rub the outside of the roast thoroughly. Wrap roast in brown paper. Place roast in 12 x 10 x 6 roasting pan. Add onions, carrots, celery, and garlic to the bottom of the pan Pour beef stock into pan until it covers ¾ of the roast. Place in oven and cook until internal temperature reaches 160 degrees, or until the outside of the roast begins to fall apart. This usually takes 4 – 6 hours at a minimum. It may take longer depending on the calibration of your home oven. Slice or shred tender beef into beef stock and serve over hot homemade biscuits. You must serve this dish HOT.

Mother's famous debris biscuit.

Mother's Beef Stock (pour over roast)

8 pounds of beef bones
2 cups vegetable oil
2 tablespoons of tomato puree
1 ½ cups of red wine
3 cups of onion quartered
1 cup carrots quartered
3 heads of garlic halved
1 ½ cups of whole mushrooms
1 tablespoon of peppercorns
2 bay leaves
6 sprigs of parsley

Preheat oven to 350F.

Place bones in roasting pan and coat with vegetable oil. Place in 350 degree oven and roast bones turning several times, cook until golden brown (be sure not to burn).

Remove bones and pour off the grease. Place pan on stove top burner and heat, add ½ cup of red wine to deglaze pan. Add roasted bones to stockpot and add water and bring to a boil. Reduce heat to a simmer then skim. After two hours add vegetables, remainder of red wine, return to a simmer and skim. Add parsley, thyme, peppercorns, and bay leaves. Keep simmering until reduced by 1/3. Strain through a fine strainer or cheesecloth. Make sure all vegetables and particles are removed. Chill and reserve for making debris.

Mother's Buttermilk Biscuits

2 cups self-rising flour
½ teaspoon salt
2/3 cup cold buttermilk
3 tablespoons of butter

Preheat oven to 450F.

Mix flour and salt together, cut butter into flour, add buttermilk and stir in slowly until dough forms a soft ball. Kneed dough 10 to 15 times. Roll out to a ½ inch thickness. Cut with a 2 inch cookie cutter and place on greased cookie pan and bake for 10 minutes.

Natchez

The Carriage House Restaurant
401 High Street
Natchez, Mississippi
Hours: Lunch Wednesday – Sunday 11a.m. to 2:30 p.m.
Special seasonal hours call to inquire
(601) 445-5151
Biscuits served all hours

About a thousand Southern belles own The Carriage House Restaurant on the grounds of historic Stanton Hall in Natchez, Mississippi.   They are the members of the Ladies Pilgrimage Garden Club, who long ago turned the old carriage house on the landmark grounds into an elegant place to lunch.

Today the ladies own and operate the popular lunch spot, known for its petite biscuits that are served promptly to every diner. Fried chicken and classic Southern cuisine tops the menu.

Lunch and Sunday brunch at the Carriage House is an elite Southern experience, with Stanton Hall—one of the oldest antebellum homes as the backdrop. Diners often lunch and then tour the grounds.

We are lucky that the biscuit recipe is one of two recipes that Garden Club members will share.

Carriage House Biscuits

2 cups of all purpose four
¼ teaspoon salt
5 tablespoons solid vegetable shortening
¾ to 1 cup milk
4 teaspoons baking powder
1 teaspoon sugar

Preheat oven to 450F

Mix all dry ingredients in a bowl. Add shortening and cut with pastry cutter until mixture looks like coarse cornmeal, add milk and let sit until it forms a ball. Place dough on floured surface. Roll out to ¼ inch thickness, and cut with ½ inch biscuit cutter.   Placed on greased cooking sheet, and bake for 15 minutes.

Biscuits & Blues
315 Main Street
Natchez, Mississippi 39201
Lunch Tuesday – Saturday 11a.m. – 2 p.m.
Dinner Tue. – Sun. 5p.m. – 10 p.m. / 11 p.m. Saturday
Sunday Brunch 11 a.m. – 2 p.m.
Live Music Friday and Saturday night
(601) 446-9922
Biscuits served all day

At Biscuit and Blues in Natchez enjoy biscuits, music, Cajun cooking, and some of the best Memphis barbecue you can stand. Biscuit and Blues owner Peter Trosclar combines all his favorite Southern culinary delights at his restaurant and club - and that includes Southern biscuits. Each customer gets one of the show-stopping biscuits, served with apricot butter. His biscuits are tall and fabulous.

Trosclar is fortunate that his sister, Southern Chef and famed biscuit maker, Regina Charboneau, allows him to use her celebrated biscuit recipe. These biscuits are rolled, folded, rolled again, cut, and then baked to high appeal.

Regina's biscuits are also served at The Biscuit and Blues club she founded in San Francisco and at her Twin Oaks Bed and Breakfast in Natchez, Mississippi.

Regina Charbonneau is a stickler about her biscuits -- touted as one of the best you'll ever eat. Regina shares her detailed biscuit recipe. She warns that you must use the exact ingredients listed for the biscuits to taste and look just like hers. No substitutions.

Biscuit Advice: Two things will make your biscuits flaky and tall; folding the dough after it's been rolled and leaving chunks of butter in the dough.

Regina Charbonneau's Famous Biscuits

4 cups flour
¼ cup Calumet baking powder
¼ cup sugar
¾ pound Land O' Lakes salted margarine
¼ pound salted Land O' Lakes butter
1 ¾ cups buttermilk

Heat oven to 375F.

In a metal mixing bowl, add flour, baking powder, and sugar. Blend well.

Cut margarine and butter into small cubes about ½ inch. Mix with dry ingredients, and coat the margarine and butter well with the flour mixture. Add buttermilk and mix into dough. Do not over mix; there should be visible pieces of butter and margarine. That is what makes these biscuits flaky.

Flour a work space and roll out to ¾ inch thick; fold and roll again. Repeat this process two to three times until you have smooth dough. The dough will be layered with butter and margarine. Cut into two-inch rounds. Bake at 375 for 20 minutes or golden brown.

Monmouth Plantation

36 Melrose Avenue
Natchez, Mississippi, 39120
Dinner 7:30 p.m. one seating only
(601) 442-5852
Biscuits served at dinner only

The antebellum diner party at Manmouth Plantation always begins with cocktails in the study at 6:30 in the evening. After drinks and hors d'oeuvres, the party moves into the opulent dining room for a five-course candlelight dinner. An intimate group of twelve can be seated at the magnificent table, with other guests seated at tables in the surrounding parlors. Southern biscuits are part of the memorable meal as Monmouth's Executive Chef, Lanny Brasher, dreams up exotic biscuit recipes for his dinners.

Monmouth is a white-pillared mansion dating back to 1818. It's operated as a posh inn offering 30 appointed rooms, all fabulously furnished. Southern hospitality is at the forefront of service. Traditional buttermilk biscuits are served to guests for breakfast. Dinner reservations are open to the public.

Monmouth Plantation is a National Historic Landmark.

Chef Brasher prepares his dinner biscuit creations with his own flare. He customarily spices up his biscuit dough with tarragon, parmesan, cinnamon, or chili powder and cumin.

Chef Lanny offers us some biscuit guidance and shares his fabulous bacon biscuit and gravy recipe.

Biscuit Advice: Keep biscuit dough cold and don't overwork the dough. Place uncooked biscuits close together on the pan so they touch, forcing them to rise higher.

Chef Lanny

Monmouth Plantation's opulent dining room

Monmouth Bacon Biscuits

2 cups all-purpose flour
3   tablespoons Calumet baking powder
1/3 teaspoon cumin
1/3 teaspoon chili powder
1 teaspoon salt
1 teaspoon pepper
¼ cup vegetable shortening
2 strips hickory smoked bacon
¼ cup minced onion
1 garlic clove, minced
½ cup buttermilk
2 tablespoons sour cream

Cook bacon in vegetable shortening, remove bacon and add onions. Cook until onions are caramelized; add garlic, and cook for 1 minute. Remove from heat and place this shortening mixture in the freezer for about 3 hours. Meanwhile, chop bacon and reserve.

Mix flour, baking powder, cumin, chili powder, salt and pepper until well incorporated.

Cut in cold vegetables, onion, garlic and bacon flavored shortening into flour mixture. Go for a large course cornmeal appearance.

In a stainless steel bowl, make a well in the flour mixture. Add sour cream and buttermilk. Begin mixing in at the well, and then expand to incorporate all of the flour mixture only until the mixture starts to pull away from sides of bowl. Place back in freezer for 5 minutes.

On a floured surface (preferably marble) roll out dough and cover with minced bacon; then knead three times. Place back in the freezer for 5 minutes.

Place chilled dough on a floured surface, roll out and cut biscuits to desired size and place in a heated cast iron skillet coated with non-stick spray. Be sure that biscuits touch one another to help them rise. Bake until light brown.

Biscuit Gravy

1/3 cup butter or bacon drippings
1/3 cup all-purpose flour
¼ cup diced onion
¼ cup minced red bell pepper
1 minced jalapeno pepper
¼ cup good chicken stock
 8 ounce can tomato puree
salt and pepper to taste

Melt bacon drippings or butter in saucepan over medium heat, add flour, and cook until light brown.

Add diced onion, bell pepper, jalapeno, and chicken stock. Cook until sauce is smooth and well mixed. Add tomato puree, and cook until mixture becomes slightly thick. Salt and pepper to taste.

Biscuit Toppings

1 fresh avocado thinly sliced, laced with lime juice to prevent browning
1 ½ cups alfalfa sprouts
½ cup sour cream
Tabasco sauce (optional)

Place a biscuit on a plate, ladle some gravy over the biscuit, and then top with sprouts, avocados, and sour cream – Tabasco sauce if you like.

*The Early Girl Eatery fits right in with charming
Asheville, North Carolina (facing page)*

Asheville

Early Girl Eatery
8 Wall Street
Asheville, North Carolina 28801
(828) 259-9292
Hours: Mon. – Fri. 7:30 a.m. – 9 p.m.
Saturday & Sunday Brunch 9 a.m. – 3 p.m.
Biscuits served for breakfast and brunch

The Early Girl Eatery fits right into the artsy vibe of beautiful Asheville, North Carolina. This bohemian style restaurant is a local biscuit favorite and is located on a side street in the historic downtown. Biscuit eaters walk right by the open kitchen before being seated in the windowed dining room overlooking the park. If diners are lucky, they get to see the owner's dad, Robert Stehling, rolling out a batch of Southern biscuits. Biscuits at The Early Girl are served straight up, as breakfast sandwiches, with sausage gravy, or with vegan herb cream gravy.

The Early Girl prides itself on using fresh ingredients, cooking everything from scratch in true Southern tradition. Along with Southern comfort food, the menu offers plenty of vegetarian options like open-faced biscuits topped with sautéed spinach, herb cream gravy, and sliced avocado.

The biscuits here are tall and light, made with a combination of butter and shortening. Owner John Stehling and his biscuit maker and father, Robert, share their recipes and biscuit success tricks.

Biscuit Advice: John says, "Don't twist the biscuit cutter; this will crimp the edges of the biscuit, causing only the center to rise." If you cut, straight up, straight down, your biscuits will rise tall and even. John says he transforms the Early Girl biscuits into sweet potato biscuits just by adding mashed sweet potatoes before adding the milk to the recipe (just enough to mix, very little). Add cinnamon and honey and you've got something special!

Early Girl Eatery Biscuits

Four cups all-purpose flour
2 heaping tablespoons baking powder
1 teaspoon salt
2 teaspoons of sugar
2 ½ ounces of butter cold
2 ½ ounces solid shortening
1 ½ cups 2 percent milk (can use whole)

Preheat oven 425 F.

Sift all dry ingredients together. By hand, cut in butter and shortening, then and add milk and mix. Turn the dough out onto a floured surface. Spread the dough out three times its size - and fold and push five times. Roll dough out to even thickness and cut into biscuits. Place biscuits on buttered pan and bake for about 20 minutes or until light brown.

Charlotte

John's Country Kitchen
1518 Central Avenue
Charlotte, North Carolina 28205
Hours: Breakfast Mon.–Fri. 6a.m. – 11 a.m.
Lunch Mon.–Fri. 11 a.m. – 3 p.m.
(704) 333-9551
Biscuits breakfast only

Jimmy Margiotis enjoys his dual role as owner and short order cook at John's Country Kitchen in Charlotte, North Carolina. An eclectic crowd gathers at the diner to throw orders at Jimmy and watch him work the grill. In the back, Jimmy's mom, Margaret, is making buttermilk biscuits, a recipe she will not part with. Margaret won't even share any of her biscuit-making tricks!

This country diner often wins the "Best Breakfast" vote in Charlotte. Plenty of grits, gravy, and lard-laden lunches are also served. Jimmy says that for more than 30 years his family has run the place, listening to his mom's advice to never to reveal or change the recipes. She also says to resist the temptation to buy cheaper ingredients.

South Carolina

Charleston

Hominy Grill
207 Rutledge Avenue
Charleston, South Carolina 29403
Hours: open 7-days a week
Breakfast 7:30 a.m. –11 a.m.
Lunch: 11:30 a.m. – 2:30 p.m.
Dinner: M-TH 5:30 p.m. – 9:30 p.m. until 10 pm Fri. & Sat.
Brunch: Saturday & Sunday 9 a.m. – 2:30 p.m.
Biscuits served for breakfast and brunch and special orders

The Hominy Grill's Executive Chef and Owner Robert Stehling says, when he decided to open a Southern restaurant, putting homemade biscuits on the menu was a given. The Hominy Grill is housed in an 1897 old shotgun house that used to be a barbershop. The restaurant has all the charm and fantastic food you'd expect to find in Charleston. This neighborhood restaurant dishes up Southern classic food; breakfast served with biscuits and hominy grits, fried green tomato and bacon sandwiches for lunch, and grilled soft shell crab with baked cheese grits for dinner.

Chef Robert bakes about 12-hundred biscuits a week, using a combination of butter, shortening, and lard in his Southern creations. He's been known to whip up biscuits for wanting customers during "off biscuit baking" hours. Now that's Southern hospitality!

Robert has worked hard to perfect his biscuit recipe and gladly shares what he has learned.

Biscuit Advice: Robert uses cake flour and a combination of butter, lard, and shortening to make his popular biscuits. He says the mixture has to be wet, almost tacky, to produce a soft biscuit. He says place biscuits barely touching on the pan so they rise high while baking. He turns his biscuit recipe into a recipe for cobbler by substituting heavy cream for milk and adding more sugar and seasonal fruit.

Hominy Grill Biscuits

4 cups cake flour
2 tablespoons baking powder
2 teaspoons sugar
1 teaspoon salt
2 ounces cold butter
2 ounces cold shortening
1 ounce cold refined lard
1 ½ cups cold milk

Preheat oven to 425F.

Sift dry ingredients together. Cut in fat, and stir in milk (minimal stirring). Turn the dough out onto a floured surface and lightly knead – no more than 10 strokes. Roll the dough out and cut into rounds. Bake for 12-15 minutes or until brown.

(Robert Stehling is the brother of John Stehling who owns The Early Girl restaurant in Asheville, North Carolina – their dad, Robert Sr., advises both of them on their biscuit making).

Poogan's Porch

72 Queen Street
Charleston, South Carolina 29401
Hours: open 7-days a week
Breakfast: 8 a.m. – 11 p.m.
Lunch: 11:30 a.m. – 3 p.m.
Dinner: 5:30 p.m. – 9:30 p.m.
Brunch: Saturday & Sunday 9 a.m. – 3 p.m.
(843) 577-2337
Biscuits served all hours

You have to love the adventure of eating at Poogan's Porch in downtown Charleston. Not only does the famed Lowcountry cuisine restaurant serve award winning food and biscuits – it is haunted by a famous ghost - Zoe St. Amad. Zoe was an old spinster who lived and died in the Victorian house, which is now Poogan's Porch. Zoe has been known to show herself to customers and staff by knocking pictures off the walls - in what is assumed to be her quest for the love she never had. I say, she's looking to love one of Poogan's famous biscuits!

"Large, light, fluffy, and golden brown." That's how biscuit maker and Executive Pastry Chef, Nicole Anhalt, describes the Southern biscuits that come out of her kitchen. Nicole says she learned the craft of biscuit making under the tutelage of the restaurant's original Executive Chef, Isaac Vanderhorse. She says the biscuits have a free-form look because they never use mixers and bakers hand pat the dough instead of rolling it out. Poogan's biscuits are served at all meals with dishes like peanut encrusted fried catfish, down home breakfasts, and shrimp and grits.

Nicole says Poogan's biscuits are large and wonderful. She shares her biscuit making tips and Poogan's dreamy biscuit recipe.

Biscuit Advice: Nicole says, "The trick to getting a light biscuit is getting the right ratio of flour to fat." She says don't add more fat thinking it will make your biscuit more tasty - it just makes it more dense and heavy.

Poogan's Porch Buttermilk Biscuits

5 pounds	self-rising flour
1 cup	sugar
½ cup	baking powder
1 pound	shortening
½ gallon	buttermilk

Preheat oven to 350 F.

Combine fist three ingredients and mix well. Add shortening and mix well with hands until shortening is broken up into quarter-sized pieces. Add buttermilk and mix until all is incorporated. Turn out onto a floured surface and roll out to ¾ inch thickness and cut with biscuit cutter. Bake 10-15 minutes.

Summerville

Woodland's Inn
125 Parsons Road
Summerville, South Carolina 29483
Hours: open 7-days a week
Breakfast: 7 a.m. – 10 a.m.
Lunch: 11:30 a.m. – 2 p.m.
Dinner: 6 p.m. – 9 p.m.
Sunday Brunch 11:30 a.m. - 2 p.m.
(843) 875-2600
Biscuits served for lunch, dinner, and brunch

For an amazing all you can eat biscuit experience, make lunch or dinner at the Woodland's in charming Summerville a must on your "to do" biscuit list. It is Southern hospitality at its best as the biscuit server makes continuous rounds to each table to refill biscuit plates with the Woodland's hallmark cheddar and herb biscuits. The restaurant is part of the Woodland's Resort and Inn, an exclusive getaway offering luxurious appointed guest rooms and top of line dinning.

Head Pastry Chef Sheree McDowell says she started making Southern Biscuits with her grandmother when she was a little girl – and now her biscuit making at the restaurant is one of the most attention getting aspects of her job.

The Woodland's is a century-old mansion with décor reminiscent of an old plantation manor. The dinning room overlooks the terrace and bamboo garden. This is a five star dining experience and the yellow cheddar biscuits are the one constant on the menu – as entrees change daily to reflect the availability of local fresh seafood and produce.

Make note of this: customers are often given tours of the kitchen, and twice a week selected diners are given the honor of eating at a table in the kitchen. This is when you can get a ringside seat to watch the biscuit maker do her thing. Sheree says she bakes about one thousand biscuits a week – and they turn out perfect every time. Sheree willingly shares her biscuit success tricks and recipe.

Biscuit Advice: Sheree says keep your ingredients cool, especially when baking in the heat of the South. She refrigerates all of her ingredients – even the flour. She says work fast and make sure the fat doesn't melt. She uses nothing but butter in her biscuits. Sheree says, in her opinion, the flavor of butter is a better trade off for the flakiness of shortening.

Woodlands Signature Cheddar & Herb Biscuits

1 ¼ cups buttermilk
2 tablespoons chopped fresh thyme
3 cups all-purpose flour
2 tablespoons baking powder
2/3 cups (1 ½ sticks) chilled unsalted butter cut into ½ inch cubes
2 tablespoons sugar
2 teaspoons salt
2 cups packed grated yellow cheddar cheese

Preheat oven to 375° F. Mix buttermilk and thyme in small bowl; let stand 5 minutes. Whisk flour, baking powder, sugar and salt in medium bowl to blend. Add cheese and butter; rub with fingertips until mixture resembles fine meal. Add buttermilk mixture and stir until soft moist clumps form. Turn dough out onto lightly floured surface; press out to thickness of ½ inch. Using 2-inch round cookie cutter cut out biscuits.

Transfer biscuits to 2 ungreased baking sheets, spacing 2 inches apart. Bake 10 minutes. Reverse position of sheets and bake biscuits until golden brown and cooked through, about 8 minutes longer. Transfer biscuits to racks. Serve warm or at room temperatures.

*Sheree enjoys baking the Woodland's
popular yellow cheddar herb biscuits.*

81

Tennessee

Music City sounds around the world as Nashville Tennessee is the home of Southern biscuits and Gibson, the famed guitar company that manufactures hand crafted stringed instruments in all shapes and sizes. Like this guitar, wonderfully named the "Biscuit," sold under Gibson's Epiphone division. It's a single resonator guitar used by many Bluegrass artists. Called the "Biscuit" because the bridge of the instrument resembles the shape of a biscuit. Gibson is mostly known for it's famous Les Paul electric guitar. But like the Southern biscuit, each Gibson guitar is unique, made for the love of music. These world class guitars feed the souls of musicians looking for that certain sound. The Biscuit guitar does that—as the "biscuit bridge" resonator results in a different flavor sound than the traditional single cone spider bridge resonator guitar.

Bon Aqua

Beacon Light
6276 Highway 100
Lyles, TN 37098
Hours: Tuesday – Friday 4 p.m. - 10 p.m.
Saturday & Sunday 9am-10pm
(931) 670-3880
Biscuits served all hours

The Beacon Light Tearoom has been beckoning biscuit lovers from around the world since it opened in 1936. Located in tiny Bon Aqua outside of Nashville near Lyles Tennessee, this out of the way—well worth the trip—biscuit eatery was featured in the documentary, *The Rise of the Southern Biscuit.* The restaurant's name was coined after the government-built beacon light that used to be located across the road. The revolving light once signaled prop lanes flying mail between Memphis and Nashville in the 1930's.

At the filming of the documentary, Don Luna, was the long time owner of the Beacon Light. His religious art adorns the walls creating a holy vibe that customers find welcoming. They also find his crisp lard biscuits and homemade preserves a blessed treat. At his retirement, Don passed his biscuit making tradition on to his Cousin Kim Winn and her husband Darrell when they bought the Beacon Light, keeping it all in the family. The Southern menu is the same; country ham, biscuits, red eye gravy, fried chicken and eggs "how you like 'em" are on the menu.

Don and his cousin Kim are most generous in sharing the Beacon Light's biscuit recipe, which was kept secret for more than 40 years. They say the key ingredient is lard, lard, lard.

Biscuit Advice: Use highly filtered hog lard. High quality lard is pure white in color and smooth in texture. The Beacon uses lard as the fat in the biscuit dough the secret is to not stop there. Melt some and brush it on the pan before placing your unbaked biscuits and them slather another coat on top before popping them into a hot hot oven. This makes the biscuits crisp on the bottom and tops and tender inside!

Beacon Light Biscuits

3 ¾ cups of sifted all-purpose flour
¼ cup of white lard
2 cups of buttermilk

Preheat oven to 475F

Sift flour into large bowl then chip the lard into the flour and blend until lard is the size of an eraser.

Turn the dough out onto a floured surface and turn it three to four times. Roll the dough to a ½ inch thickness and cut into two-inch rounds. Place on a baking pan that's been liberally brushed with melted lard. After placing the biscuits, brush the tops with melted lard, and put immediately into a hot oven for 10 minutes. Tops should get toasted brown.

Don Luna standing in front of some of his religious art collection holds a plate of his fabulous lard biscuits topped with the homemade preserves of the day. He smiles, saying biscuit fan who saw him in the documentary thought he said "It's the Lord that makes the biscuits" instead of "It's the lard that makes the biscuits."

Chattanooga

Aretha Frankensteins
518 Treemont Street
Chattanooga, Tennessee
Hours: 7 a.m. to midnight daily
(423) 265-7685
Biscuits served all day

Hip and cool - "THE" place to be seen in North Chattanooga and the only place around where you can grab a beer and gargantuan Southern biscuit.

Aretha Frankensteins is the dream child of owner, Jeff Brakebill, who renovated a dilapidated house in an unseemly neighborhood of Chattanooga - all to open his fantasy restaurant. The fix-up took three years and all the while he made hundreds of biscuits in his home kitchen trying to come up the perfect recipe.

Jeff says he kneads his biscuit dough more than other biscuit makers - but he likes how his turn out. Jeff's biscuit pancake, and waffle recipes are his own. His place is packed all day, every day, with thousands of sugar-dusted biscuits gobbled down weekly.

Aretha Frankensteins atmosphere is eclectic—Mosaic tiles and wood-beamed ceilings are the backdrop for these knockout biscuits.

Jeff named his restaurant after a flip joke he made at a Halloween party years ago. When he walked up to the party, he saw a wreath on the door decorated with little Frankensteins. "A wreath of Frankensteins," he commented. Everyone laughed and the restaurant was named "Aretha Frankensteins" in spirit of the joke.

Jeff is good-natured and kind enough to cut down his large biscuit recipe for this printing. He and actually tested it to make sure it would be perfect.

Aretha Frankenstiens Biscuits

6 cups all purpose flour
1 ½ tablespoons salt
5 tablespoons sugar
5 tablespoons baking powder
2 sticks butter
2 2/3 cups buttermilk

Preheat oven to 300F.

Mix dry ingredients in a big bowl. Cut butter in by hand then add buttermilk. Use a spatula to mix wet dough until it is basically a dough ball.

Remove dough ball, and knead about 10 times on a floured surface. Roll into 1 inch thick, and cut with a pint glass. Place biscuits on cookie sheet, and lightly dust with sugar. Bake at 300 degrees for 20 minutes.

Jeff's stunning biscuits are so awesome; they've been featured on the Food Network.

Franklin

Dotson's
99 East Main Street
Franklin, Tennessee
Monday-Friday 7 a.m. – 8:30 p.m.
Saturday and Sunday 7 a.m. – 2:30 p.m.
(615) 794-2805
Biscuits served all day

For a genuine Southern meat and three experience, head to Dotson's in Franklin Tennessee. This down home country restaurant has been turning out good times and even better cooking since the 1950's. As you walk towards the door, the smell of fried chicken and homemade goodies fill the air – a prelude of what's to come. Mashed potatoes, green beans, meatloaf, chicken and dumplings, and cream pies are standard offerings. Fresh baked lard biscuits served with Dotson's country breakfasts and throughout the day. Dotson's biscuits are a middle Tennessee favorite.

Dotson's key Biscuit Maker is Janet Garner. Janet shares the recipe and her favorite biscuit making tip.

Biscuit Advice: Janet says brush the biscuit pan with butter and make sure that you don't add too much flour to the dough in the rolling out stage.

Dotson's Buttermilk Lard Biscuits

6 cups of all-purpose flour
½ cup solid vegetable
shortening
¼ cup sugar
1 teaspoon of baking powder
3 cups of buttermilk

Preheat oven to 350F.

Combine buttermilk, shortening, sugar, and baking powder.
Add flour slowly, mixing continuously. Roll dough out on a
lightly floured surface to ¾ inch thickness. Butter the pan
with melted butter. Cut biscuits with a lightly floured cutter.
Brush tops with butter. Bake for 20 minutes

Merridee's Breadbasket
110 Fourth Avenue South
Franklin, TN 37064
Hours: 7 a.m.-5 p.m. Mon.–Sat.; Lunch 10:30 a.m. until 5 p.m.
Treats 7 a.m. until 5 p.m.
(615) 790-3755
Biscuits served for breakfast

Merridee's Breadbasket, a picturesque Southern
bakery/restaurant, offers every bit of lovin' from the oven you
can imagine – including large fresh biscuits! Merridee's is
located off the square of historic Franklin and is worth a visit
not only for baked goods, but to experience the beautiful town
it calls home. Merridee's large yummy biscuits were featured
in the documentary, ***The Rise of the Southern Biscuit.***

Every tasty treat that comes out of Merridee's oven is made from scratch, no preservatives allowed. That includes large Southern biscuits made with heavy cream. Glance into Merridee's bakery case and see legions of biscuits, breads, pastries, and pies. So hard to choose!

Merridee's biscuits are served plain, with sausage gravy, or made into giant breakfast sandwiches. Here's the recipe and some tips.

Biscuit Advice: Biscuit maker and owner of Merridee's Marylin Kreider says she and her bakers put a new twist on their biscuits by adding tasty ingredients; like ham, raisins, and spices – to switch things up!

Merridee's Southern Biscuits

1 lb. of cake flour
1 oz. baking powder
¾ oz. granulated sugar
Pinch of salt
½ oz. butter
1/3 c. heavy cream

Preheat oven to 400F.

Place dry ingredients together in bowl, and cut butter until mixture resembles course cornmeal. Add cream and mix just until moistened.

*Marylin Krieder,
owner of Merridee's
holds her glazed topped
cinnamon raisin
biscuits with glaze!*

Turn the dough out onto a floured surface, roll, and cut. Place on ungreased pan, and bake for 20 minutes.

Miss Daisy's Kitchen
2176 Hillsboro Road
Franklin, TN 37069
Hours: 8a.m. –7 p.m. 7 days a week
(615) 599-5313
Biscuits served all day

Miss Daisy's Kitchen is tucked away in the corner of the
Grassland Market in Franklin, Tennessee. Behind the
colorful counter you'll find an array of delicious home
cooked food, and of course, classic Southern biscuits.
Southern culinary treasure, Miss Daisy King is the expert on
Southern food and hospitality. Miss Daisy is featured in ***The
Rise of the Southern Biscuit.*** Her market-kitchen offers
daily specials that can be eaten at small tables next to the
counter, or you can order food on the run. Dream up any
special request for a party or get together, order ahead, and
Miss Daisy gets it done. Miss Daisy is famous for her five
flavor pound cake, a recipe she inherited from her mother.

She is also a biscuit expert and very open to sharing her
wonderful recipes. Below are Miss Daisy's traditional
buttermilk biscuit recipe and her angel biscuit recipe.

Angel biscuits, she says, were often called "brides biscuits"
in the Old South. Even the most inexperienced baker can
make these biscuits rise with confidence. That's because the
recipe calls for yeast, baking powder, and baking soda.

Biscuit Advice: Miss Daisy says, "Biscuits have many legs,
serve them alone, for breakfast, as a sandwich, with a
topping, or as a dessert."

Angel biscuits are wonderful because the dough contains yeast and can be prepared ahead of time and stored for days in the refrigerator.

Miss Daisy's Traditional Biscuits

1 cup all-purpose flour
2 teaspoons baking powder
¼ teaspoon salt
¼ teaspoon baking soda
2 ½ tablespoons vegetable shortening or butter
½ cup buttermilk

Preheat oven to 450F.

In a deep bowl sift dry ingredients; cut in shortening or butter. Add buttermilk all at once and stir into a ball of dough. Knead lightly. Roll out onto a floured board to a ½ inch thickness. Cut with biscuit cutter. Place on baking sheet and bake in a 450F oven for 10 to 12 minutes. Yield: 12 biscuits.

Miss Daisy's Angel Biscuits

5cups all-purpose flour
4 tablespoons sugar
1 tablespoon baking powder
1 teaspoon salt
1 teaspoon baking soda
¾ cup butter
1 envelope dry yeast
3 tablespoons warm water
2 cups buttermilk
1/8 cup melted butter.

Preheat oven to 400F.

In a deep bowl sift all dry ingredients: cut in butter with fork or pastry blender until mixture is crumbly.

Dissolve yeast in water. Stir yeast and buttermilk into flour mixture, mix until dough ball forms.

Roll out onto a floured board to a ½ inch thickness. Cut with biscuit cutter. Brush with melted butter. Place on baking sheet and bake in a 400-degree oven for 10 to 12 minutes or until golden brown. Yield: 24 to 36 biscuits depending on the size of your biscuit cutter.

Here's Miss Daisy holding a fresh batch of her angel biscuits. The glass rolling pin was inherited by Daisy from her mother.

Lynchburg

Miss Mary Bobo's Boarding House
Lynchburg, Tennessee 37352
Hours: Monday-Saturday, Lunch seating only 1:00 p.m.
Family Style Dining Reservations Required
(931) 759-7394
Biscuits served all hours

Miss Mary Bobo's Boarding House is located just off the town square of Lynchburg, Tennessee. Reservations are highly suggested as many biscuit eaters travel to Miss Mary Bobo's to experience a traditional Southern family style meal. Large tables are seated with a mix of guests and a Southern hostess who initiates conversation and makes introductions.

The old boarding house started as a traveler's hotel in 1867. Miss Mary ran the boarding until her death at age 102 in 1983.

Today Lynn Tolley runs and operates Miss Mary Bobo's and prides herself on keeping the Southern biscuit tradition alive. Lynn serves a standard baking powder biscuits every day, with Ham cup muffin biscuits, and cornmeal biscuits as specials.

Miss Mary Bobo's Baking Powder Biscuits

2 cups self-rising flour
½ teaspoon salt
3   teaspoons of baking powder
6 tablespoons butter or shortening
¾ cup milk

Preheat oven to 450F.

In a bowl, sift flour with the baking powder and salt. Cut in the butter or shortening (or a combination of the two) until the mixture resembles coarse meal. Stir the milk into the mixture until the dough forms a ball.

Turn the dough onto a lightly floured surface and knead several times. Roll with floured rolling pin to a ½ inch thickness. Cut with biscuit cutter or small glass. Place on ungreased cookie sheet. Bake for 10 to 15 minutes, or until lightly browned. Makes 12 two-inch biscuits.

Miss Mary Bobo's Cornmeal Biscuits

1 ½ cups sifted self-rising flour
¾ cup cornmeal
¼ teaspoon baking soda
3   teaspoons baking powder
1 teaspoon salt
1 tablespoon sugar
4   tablespoons butter
1 egg beaten
½ cup buttermilk or sour milk butter

Preheat oven to 450F.

Sift dry ingredients together. Cut in the butter. Mix egg with buttermilk then add to dry ingredients. Turn onto a floured board knead lightly. Roll out to a ½ inch thickness. Cut with a biscuit cutter. Brush with butter and fold over into half-moon shape. Bake for 12 to 15 minutes or until golden. Makes 24 biscuits.

Miss Mary Bo Bo's Muffin Cup Ham Biscuits

2 cups self-rising flour
1 cup milk
½ cup mayonnaise
2 cups chopped country ham

Heat oven to 425F. Grease 12 regular or 24 mini muffin cups.

Combine all ingredients in a large mixing bowl. Stir with fork to make soft dough. Drop spoonfuls into the greased muffin cups. Bake until golden brown about 15 minutes for regular muffin cups, 8-10 minutes for mini muffin cups

Memphis

Barksdale's
237 South Cooper
Memphis, Tennessee 38104
Hours: Monday – Friday 7 a.m. – 2 p.m.
Breakfast all day Saturday & Sunday 7 a.m. – 2 p.m.
(901) 722-2193
Biscuits served breakfast only Mon. – Fri.
Biscuits served all weekend

Barksdale's is a self-proclaimed "no-frills hole-in-the wall" Southern diner. Biscuit maker and owner Bob Henry made his first biscuit as a boy then grew up to make a career out of biscuit making – creating winning biscuit combinations for big-time chain restaurants.

In 2000, Bob went into the biscuit business for himself when he bought the long established Barkdale's in Memphis. This is where Bob's love of biscuit making found an appreciative home. Bob can be seen in the kitchen rolling out his homemade biscuits. His pancakes and even the syrup he serves are homemade, as well. His biscuits are served hot and topped with white gravy.

Bob makes his creations with his brand of "biscuit insurance", putting combinations of the best ingredients into his well-thought-out biscuit.

Bob measures ingredients with his hands, so there are no measurements to share, but Bob will dish this.

Biscuit Advice: Use a light colored baking pan for golden brown biscuit bottoms. Dark pans turn biscuit bottoms dark.

Try mixing combinations of the same types of ingredients to achieve the taste you want. For example, mix combinations of butter, shortening, and lard for the fat in your biscuit. Or mix whole milk with buttermilk, or with water or heavy cream to achieve a unique tasting biscuit.

Barkdale's Biscuit Ingredients

Self-rising flour
A combination of lard, butter, and shortening
salt and baking powder
buttermilk
whole milk

Blue Plate Cafe
5469 Poplar
Memphis, TN 38119
Hours open daily 6 a.m. – 8 p.m
(901) 761-9696
Biscuits served all hours

When you sit down at the Blue Plate Café in Memphis, a basket of hot biscuits served with a side of white sausage gravy is one of the first things to hit the table. This café is famous for its all-day, HUGE, HEARTY Southern biscuits. Owner Mike Richmond dedicates one biscuit maker to keep the Blue Plate in biscuits. He estimates that up to 10-thousand biscuits are served daily at his restaurant's three locations.

Along with the biscuits and gravy, each breakfast is served with hash browns and homemade pancakes. At lunchtime, cornbread joins the basket of biscuits and gravy. Mike Richmond laughs when he talks about how full and sleepy his customers are when they leave, a true compliment to the cook!

Everything on the country cooking menu is made fresh. Mike is proud to report that there are only two canned items in his kitchen, canned cranberry sauce, because customers like it better than homemade, and fruit cocktail, vital to the Jell-O.

Mike's been making biscuits since he was a kid and clues us in on how it's done. His biscuits are laced with a combination of rich and sweet ingredients. Because of the volume of business, Blue Plate biscuits are made up in batches with 250 pounds of flour. For that reason, we don't have exact measurements, but Mike shares the ingredients he uses, and his biscuit making technique.

Biscuit Advice: Mike puts sugar in his biscuit recipe. He says if you're not careful, high heat will crystallize the sugar and turn your biscuits too crisp and brown. His trick for keeping his biscuits soft and white is to bake them at a lower temperature of 325F.

Fold, do not knead, dough. The more you work the dough, the less your biscuits will rise.

Blue Plate Biscuits Ingredients

Self-rising flour
shortening
sugar
buttermilk
whole milk
eggs

Preheat oven to 325 F.

Mix self-rising flour and shortening until it resembles course cornmeal. Add eggs and equal parts of buttermilk and whole milk to the flour. Stir the mixture until it gets wet and sticky. Let the mixture stand until it forms a dough ball.

Turn the dough ball out onto a floured surface and fold a few times; roll out and cut biscuits out with a glass.

Bake at 325F for 8 minutes or until done.

There are two other Blue Plate Café's - one Court South in Memphis, the other in Bartlett, Kentucky, on Kirby Whitten Road.

Bryant's Breakfast

3965 Summer Avenue
Memphis, TN 38122
Hours: open daily 5 a.m. – 1 p.m.
(901) 324-7494
Biscuits served all day

Grabbing biscuits and breakfast at Bryant's in Memphis is habit forming for early risers who are treated like family at this long standing eatery. Brother and sister Phil and Kerrie Bryant are carrying on a 30-year tradition started by their father when he opened the diner. Breakfast combinations are served with trios of homemade buttermilk biscuits and gravy.

Regulars are called by name when they walk through the door and most of their orders are memorized by the wait staff.

The Bryant biscuit recipe is a secret, but Phil does share some interesting tips on how he makes his biscuits.

Biscuit Advice: Phil insists on baking his biscuits in a home oven. He says commercial convection ovens dry out his biscuits.

Bake your biscuits fast at 500 degrees and rotate the pan half way during the baking process.

Broil the tops of biscuits with butter just before taking them out of the oven to give them a crisp finish.

Buns on the Run

2150 Elzey Avenue
Memphis, TN 38104
Hours: 7a.m. – 2 p.m. Tuesday – Friday
Closed Sunday & Monday
(901) 278-2867
Biscuits served all hours

Buns on the Run is a biscuit/breakfast favorite for Memphis locals who enjoy the friendly charm of the clapboard bakery cafe. Homemade treats like breads, cakes, and pies galore are stacked beautifully in the bakery case. All goodies are made from scratch daily – and that includes hot, fresh Southern biscuits.

Breakfast and lunch are served in the cozy dining area that seats 30. Owners Pam Hardin and Sharron Johnson met as PTA moms in 1997 and decided to put their love of baking into a business. Their bungalow bakery was written up in *National Geographic's Travel Guide*. The Buns biscuit recipe is simply foolproof. Here's the biscuit recipe and tips.

Biscuit Advice: Sharron says the sides of your cookie or baking sheet matter. If you want crispy biscuits, use a pan with no sides. If you want a softer biscuit, use a pan that has sides.

Bake biscuits alone in the oven. Baking them with other food causes condensation. Sharron says it can make your biscuits sweaty! Yuck.

Bun's on the Run Biscuits

2 cups self-rising flour
¼ cup of shortening
¾ cup of 2 percent milk

Preheat oven to 450F.

Put flour in bowl, and cut in shortening.   Add milk and mix to form a sticky dough.

Turn the sticky dough onto a floured board and turn it over just one time to coat with flour.

Pat or roll the dough out to a ½ inch thickness – DO NOT KNEAD.

Cut biscuits out and place on greased pan

Bake at 450 for 12 to 15 minutes. Yields 8 biscuits

Nashville /Music City

Cabana
1910 Belcourt Avenue
Nashville, TN 37212
Hours: 4 p.m. – 3 a.m. Monday –Saturday
Sunday 4 p.m. – midnight
(615) 577-2262
Biscuits served all hours

If a Southern biscuit can be chic, Executive Chef and owner of Cabana in Hillsboro Village, has done the most fashionable job. Cabana's sweet potato biscuits are in vogue and delicious. Plates of the orange biscuits sandwiched with stacks of paper-thin country ham and fried chicken keep highballs and martinis company at this trendy nightspot.

Chef Brian Uhl puts his own up scale twist on Southern comfort food by using ingredients native to Tennessee. Buttermilk fried chicken, trout, lobster brie macaroni and cheese are a few of the dishes that come out of Uhl's kitchen—along with those sweet potato biscuits, country ham, and homemade peach preserves.

Cabana is a stylish social scene with a feeling of down home hospitality—the biscuits have everything to do with sending that friendly message.

Chef Uhl shares his sweet potato biscuit recipe and his tips for biscuit making success.

Biscuit Advice: When adding your fat into the flour, try not to overwork the mixture. Once you overwork the mixture, you'll get a heavy biscuit.

Turn this sweet potato biscuit into dessert by adding cinnamon and pecans.

Cabana Sweet Potato Biscuits

6 cups all-purpose flour
2 tablespoons baking powder
1 ½ teaspoons of baking soda
1 tablespoon salt
1 tablespoon sugar
1 cup plus 1 tablespoon unsalted butter (cold)
1 cup plus 1 tablespoon shortening (cold)
3 cups pureed baked sweet potatoes peeled
1 cup of half and half

Preheat oven 425F.

Sift all dry ingredients together and put them into a food processor.

Cut cold butter into small cubes and place in the food processor with the dry mixture. Pulse a few times until the butter just breaks up. Add the cold shortening and pulse until the mixture resembles course cornmeal. *Be careful not over-pulse the mixture. The friction will cause the butter and shortening to melt, and your biscuits will not turn out as fluffy.*

Transfer mixture to mixing bowl and fold in sweet potatoes. As you fold, a dough ball will form. Now add the half and half, which should turn the dough very wet.

Add flour in small amounts to offset dough that's too wet. *The dough should be wet but not sticky.*

On a floured surface, roll the dough out to a ½- ¾ inch thickness. Cut the biscuits into rounds.

Place biscuits on a greased sheet pan and bake for 4 minutes. Then rotate the pan and bake for another 4 minutes for a total of 8 minutes.

Brush fresh baked biscuits with hot melted butter.

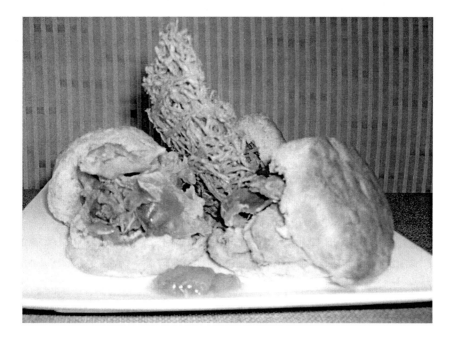

Cabana sweet potato biscuits with shaved country ham.

G & W Hamery
411 West Lytle Street
Murfreesboro Tennessee 37130
(615) 893-9712
Hours: Mon.-Fri   9 a.m. – 5 p.m.
During Holidays open Saturday 9 a.m. – 2:00 p.m.
Ham biscuits available for pick up must call ahead please.

I loved my visit to the G & W Hamery in Murfreesboro, Tennessee. I felt like I was entering a hobbit house as I walked through the Hamery door. It's down around back and down a few steps into a cellar. A cellar filled with country hams, angel biscuits, and Southern hospitality. There you will find owner Bob Woods and his assistant JP Perry slicing deboned smoked country ham amongst trays of homemade biscuits. Bob's biscuit maker, Ruth, bakes pans of the small angel biscuits to complement the country ham. Locals call ahead and order ham biscuits for business meetings, parties, and picnics.

Bob works where he played as a boy when the space used to be his grandfather's veterinary hospital, of all things. Bob says, His uncles' would cure hams and sell them to customers as a hobby. He learned their sugar curing secrets, and now runs a full time country ham and biscuit business out of the small space.   Bob's small ham biscuits are split and stuffed with stacks of his thinly sliced award-winning country ham. For holidays, he sells gift boxes and baskets and countless pick up orders. His assistant, J.P. Perry cans her own fresh vegetables from her truck farm and sells them at the ham store as well.

Here's Bob and J.P. with a pan of Angel Biscuits and thinly sliced country ham.

Bob is friendly and always willing to chat with customers about Southern food and the good old days in Murfreesboro. He's glad to show you around his hamery, even open one of the nearby doors to his ham cellars so you can see his wonderful hams hanging. Make sure you call ahead so they can get your order ready. You've got to love that a cut-off tail pipe from a nearby auto parts store is what they use as a biscuit cutter!

Here's Bob's biscuit recipe and a perhaps one of the best biscuit tips of the book.

Biscuit tip: Bob freezes his raw biscuits, then thaws and bakes when he needs them. He says they taste fresh. The most homemade frozen biscuit if there ever was one.

*Bob's biscuits with the cut off tail pipe he uses
as his biscuit cutter.*

G & W Hamery Angel Biscuit Recipe

4 cups flour
1 ¾ cups buttermilk
¾ cup shortening
¼ tsp baking soda
2 tsp. yeast
2tsp. sugar
1 cup water

Mix buttermilk and baking soda together and let it stand
Mix yeast and warm water together and let it stand
Mix flour and shortening together until shortening is eraser
size and then add in the buttermilk/soda and water/yeast
mixtures and form mixture into a dough and let it rise. After

dough rises roll out on a floured surface and cut and place on pan.

Bake at 350 degrees for about 8 minutes or until golden brown.

Hachland Hill Vineyard
5396 Rawlings Road
Joelton, TN
Hours: open 7 days a week
(615) 876-8181
Biscuits served on demand

For the ultimate in Southern hospitality join chef and cookbook author Phila Hach for dinner, lunch, or an overnight visit at her Hachland Hill Vineyard or Spring Creek Inn, nestled in Joelton, Tennessee. Phila cooks spectacular Southern meals for intimate and large groups that desire an "Inn-like" setting for a special occasion.

Phila was featured in the documentary *The Rise of the Southern Biscuit* as she made a batch of beaten biscuits, one of the oldest biscuit recipes of the South. Phila is a believer in biscuits. She always whips up biscuits while her guests are eating their salads. "Biscuits are fast, delightful, and wonderful," exclaims Phila. She shares her favorite buttermilk biscuit recipe, and two versions (one is her grandmother's) of the old time beaten biscuit recipe she calls, "an old acquaintance not forgotten". As bonus she offers a recipe for Southern chocolate gravy, a recipe that emerged during the civil war when meat was scarce.

Biscuit Advice: Phila dissolves her baking soda into the buttermilk before adding it to the flour. She says this way the soda gets more evenly distributed throughout the dough.

Phila says anyone can make a biscuit. She suggests you start by using all-purpose flour, a liquid, and a fat. Once you get that down you're on your way.

Phila advises, "biscuits like love should be in every home".

Watch Phila bake her famous sugar biscuits in the bonus footage www.theriseofthesouthernbiscuit.com

Phila's Favorite Buttermilk Biscuits

1 cup of buttermilk with a pinch of baking soda
2 cups flour
1 teaspoon salt
2 heaping teaspoons of baking powder
1 heaping tablespoon of lard, the size of a large egg

Preheat oven to 450F.

Put pinch of baking soda into buttermilk and let stand for a minute. Meanwhile, mix dry ingredients in a mixing bowl. Dump in lard and buttermilk with soda into the flour and stir quickly, about 30 seconds. Turn the dough out onto a floured board and fold about 10 times. Pat the dough out into a ½ inch thick disc and cut with a small biscuit cutter. Bake in a 450-degree oven until golden brown.

Phila's Beaten Biscuits

4   cups sifted flour
1 cup hog lard
1 teaspoon salt
1 tablespoon sugar
1 teaspoon baking powder
1 ½ cups ice cold milk

Preheat oven to 350F.

Sift flour, baking powder, salt, and sugar three times. Using your finger tips cut in the lard until the mixture becomes fine. Add the cold milk to make stiff dough.

Beat the dough out flat, fold and beat again and again until it is smooth, glossy and full of blisters. This will take about a half hour or 400 strokes.

Finally roll out the dough to a ½ inch thickness. Cut with small cutter then prick biscuits through with a fork to hold the flaky layers together. Do not add any additional flour when rolling out. Bake at 350-degrees for approximately 30 minutes. Yield: 8 dozen small biscuits.

Phila's Grandmother's Beaten Biscuits
(This is an old-time basic recipe that was used in the first days of the Old South)

4 cups flour (not sifted)
1 teaspoon salt
¼ pound lard
cold water

Mix flour, lard and salt with hands until cornmeal like consistency. Add cold water until dough is stiff and does not stick to hands.

Separate dough into two parts. Beat and fold each section hundreds of times by either running it through the biscuit break, or by beating it with a beaten biscuit mallet.

When the dough looks smooth and feels like velvet roll out to ½ inch thickness and cut into small rounds. Prick each biscuit with a fork three times to hold the flaky layers together. Bake at 300 degrees for 45 minutes. Open the oven when finished to let the biscuits dry out. Serve with country ham. You can store unused biscuits in a tin for a long shelf life.

Chocolate Gravy

(Phila says cooks during the civil war came up with chocolate gravy for their biscuits when meat became scarce during wartime. She made chocolate gravy over biscuits for me -- then when we were done, she turned the gravy into a chocolate pie by adding three eggs to the gravy and baking it in a pie shell for 20 minutes. Yummy!!!)

butter the size of a small egg
¼ cup coco
¼ cup sugar
½ cup milk or water
½ teaspoon vanilla (optional)

Mix the ingredients together in sauce pan then simmer over low heat until gravy thickens. Serve over biscuits.

Loveless Café

8400 Highway 100
Nashville, TN
Hours: 7a.m. – 9 p.m. 7 days a week
(615) 646-9700
Biscuits served all day

The Loveless Café located just outside of Music City and is a famed biscuit restaurant with an even more famous biscuit maker, Carol Fay.

Biscuits, breakfast, smoked barbecue, fried chicken, country ham, and red eye gravy are on the menu. Yet, the biscuits and celebrity biscuit maker Carol Fay are the stars of the Loveless.

This biscuit hot spot was once the Loveless Motel and Café, owned by Annie Loveless who served biscuits and fried chicken out of her house to passersby. It's still going on.

Today the old house has been renovated to a homey eatery where biscuits and preserves are the centerpiece of each table. Biscuit fans line up to feed on the Loveless experience.

It's fun to watch Carol Fay make her secret recipe in the "Biscuit Window" where she seamlessly cranks out pans of biscuits. It's amazing to watch. She stops, gets her picture taken, and signs a few autographs with her biscuit fans.

*Carol Fay talks about her biscuit making heritage in the documentary **The Rise of the Southern Biscuit.***

Carol's biscuits are moist and dense. She's been making Loveless biscuits for more than 20 years. She will not part with her secret biscuit recipe but will share how to make the famous preserves she serves with her biscuits. No thickeners used here. Just stir, stir, and stir.

115

Strawberry Preserves

5   cups of strawberries (fresh or frozen)
1 cup of sugar
½ teaspoon of salt

Gently rinse the strawberries in cold water. Set them in the sink to dry. Trim the tops off the berries and cut the berries in half. Put the berries in a large pot with the sugar and salt. Let sit for 2 hours or until strawberries release their juices. Bring the strawberries to a simmer on medium heat for 30 to 45 minutes. Gently stir: cook the berries until reduced by half or the mixture reaches jam thickness. Jar the preserves right out of the kettle, filling each jar to the top. Place a top on each jar as tight as possible.

Here's Carol Fay stirring her preserves.

Martha Stamps Catering and Events
Nashville, Tennessee
(615) 353-2828
Biscuits available by pre-order

Martha Stamps is a well known as an upscale Southern chef and cookbook author based in Nashville, Tennessee. Martha holds everything Southern near and dear to her heart— including the homemade biscuit. You can see Martha in *The Rise of the Southern Biscuit* making beaten biscuits on her family heirloom electric biscuit break—driven by a sewing machine motor. Small motors were added to the old fashioned hand crank machines in an effort to modernize the laborious task of making beaten biscuits. Martha loves them because they are hard to come by, and she still makes them for her family and friends.

Martha's culinary career path has moved on from restaurateur to catering. Her scallion biscuits were a staple at her former restaurant, Martha's at the Plantation located at the historic Belle Meade Plantation. Her biscuits are petite and engineered to have more shelf life than a buttermilk biscuit. Even though Martha loves all biscuits and bakes many, she loves the staying power of her scallion biscuits. For those who've eaten them and loved them, nice to know you can still order them from Martha.

Martha shares her reputable scallion biscuit recipe and her biscuit making advice.

Biscuit Advice: Buttermilk versus heavy cream. If you're going to serve biscuits right away, use buttermilk.

Buttermilk biscuits are great hot and fresh but can't be kept waiting. If you have to make your biscuits up ahead of time or they need to last all day, use heavy cream. Cream biscuits have staying power.

Use your fingertips when incorporating, lard, butter, or shortening in biscuits. The palms of your hands have more heat and melt the fat which leads to a flatter biscuit.

Martha's Scallion Biscuits

2 cups flour
1 tablespoon plus ¾ teaspoon baking powder
½ teaspoon salt
2 ½ teaspoons of sugar
1 stick cold unsalted butter, cut into bits
3 eggs, beaten
1/3 cup heavy cream
1 scallion, green and white parts, sliced thin

Preheat oven to 350F.

Mix dry ingredients together in a food processor. Add diced butter, and pulse until mixture resembles coarse cornmeal.

Move mixture to a bowl and mix in cream, eggs, and scallion. Roll out to ½ inch thick, and cut into small rounds. Bake for 10 minutes.

Martha's petite scallion biscuits are her signature biscuit very popular in Nashville.

Monell's

1235 6th Ave N
Nashville, TN 37208
No Reservations accepted, Family Style Service
Lunch Monday thru Friday 10:30 a.m – 2 p.m.
Dinner Tuesday-Saturday 5:00 a.m. - 8:30 p.m.
Country Breakfast Saturday and Sunday 8:30 a.m. -11a.m.
(615) 248-4747
Biscuits served all day

Monell's is a grand Victorian home located in Nashville's Historic German Town and is a favorite spot for Southern style lunches and suppers in Music City. The family-style dining is just like eating at grandma's—with platters and bowls passing around the table—as well as good conversation. Owner Michael King says homemade biscuits are one of the few constant items on his menu. Monell's menu changes daily from one Southern delight to another. Chicken and dumplings, pan fried chicken, mashed potatoes, deviled eggs, and corn pudding just begin to tell the tasty story.

Guests are seated together at large dining tables. Meeting new people is all part of the wonderful Southern experience at Monell's. So don't be shy and remember—pass those biscuits to the left.

To find out what's cooking, just call Monell's, and they'll tell you what's on the table for that day.

Biscuit Advice: Michael King says, "The less you handle the dough, the better the biscuits. Make your own buttermilk by mixing ½ tsp. of vinegar in whole milk."

A smile and bottomless baskets of Southern biscuits are staples at Monell's.

Strangers become new friends as guests at Monell's sit together and pass the biscuits to the left.

Monell's Country Biscuits

2 cups all-purpose flour
½ teaspoon salt
¼ teaspoon baking soda
1 tablespoon baking powder
½ cup vegetable shortening – solid shortening
1 cup buttermilk (room temperature)

Preheat oven to 400 F.

Sift dry ingredients together.

Mix shortening with a fork or fingertips until the mixture resembles course cornmeal.

Make a well in the center of flour mixture, and pour in room temperature buttermilk.

Incorporate flour and buttermilk until flour leaves sides of bowl and forms a ball. If it sticks, add a little more flour until it comes away from the sides of the bowl.

Place dough on floured surface, and knead five to six times. Make sure the surface is not cold.

You can roll out to ½ inch thickness and cut with a biscuit cutter; however, we use a small ice cream scoop.

Place biscuits on greased cookie sheet. Bake for 8 –12 minutes, and brush with melted butter. Yields 12 biscuits.

The Nashville Biscuit House
805 Gallatin Road
Nashville, TN 37206
(615) 228-4504
Hours: Tue. – Sat. 6:30—2:30p.m. Sun.7:30 a.m – 2:30 p.m.
Biscuits Served All Day

Southern to the core, the Nashville Biscuit House is home to "breakfast all day" and that translates to "biscuits all day" at this Music City diner. If you desire a Southern Meat and Three experience—this is it. Cozy, no frills, and eclectic describes this welcoming East Nashville eatery. When you call, the friendly wait staff answers, "The Biscuit!" And that—it is.

Here's a glance of The Nashville Biscuit House's homey feel, which includes biscuits!

Restaurant owner and Southern Cook John Colson is dedicated to preparing his food the Southern way. For him, homemade biscuits, sausage gravy, collards, and turnip greens are a must. He prides himself on the fact that very few canned goods reside in his kitchen. His biscuits are golden, almost yellow, and very appealing. He blends a combination of Crisco and butter in his biscuits. They're offered with country ham, slab bacon, as egg sandwiches, and served with his famous sausage gravy.

John says he's not going to give out his beloved biscuit recipe, but will share how to make his sausage gravy. Gravy he says people drive from miles around to get a taste of.

The Nashville Biscuit House Sausage Gravy

*Start with good sausage, John says you get what you pay for.
*Add your own spices to the sausage to make it your own; sage and pepper
*Brown the sausage in bits and let some stick to the pan, the more the better.
*Add some flour to the mixture and scrape the brown bits to form a rue.
*Add water and milk and stir the browned sausage mixture into a gravy.
*Add a lot of black pepper and invest in a good name brand.

John says almost add what you may think to be too much pepper. That when you pour the gravy over the biscuit, the starch in the biscuit creates the perfect balance.

John Colson blends Crisco and butter to create his secret biscuit recipe. He believes biscuits are best topped with peppered sausage gravy, honey, or jam. "Biscuits are the perfect culinary companion to so many other Southern foods," he says.

Texas

Austin

1886 Café and Bakery (located at Driskill Hotel)

604 Brazos Street
Austin, TX 78701
Hours: Sun.–Thu. 7 a.m. – 10 p.m. Fri. & Sat. 1 p.m.–midnight
(512) 474-5911
Biscuits served all day

The 1886 Café and Bakery is located in the historic Driskill Hotel in Austin, Texas. The bakery/Café is charming and famous for its jalapeno and corn biscuits. The recipe comes from notable Pastry Chef, A. Mark Chapman. Chef Chapman serves his corn biscuits by themselves, which are wonderful. He also uses the biscuits as the foundation for his version of eggs benedict; poached eggs smothered in chorizo gravy and topped with sliced apple bacon.

The bakery/restaurant was once the billiard parlor and telegraph room at the hotel where America's first long distance telephone call was made. The dining room includes a glass wall where customers can watch the pastry chefs at work. Chef Chapman was named one of America's top ten pastry chefs by ***Pastry Art & Design*** magazine. Chef Chapman shares his biscuit sense and fabulous jalapeno corn biscuit and chorizo gravy recipes.

Biscuit Advice: Chef Chapman says, "Make sure your dough is moist enough. My secret is to fold in whipped egg whites. This makes your dough lighter and allows you to use less baking powder."

"Take any biscuit recipe and add raisins, apricots, peanuts and corn. Be creative!"

You can see the goodness baked in Chapman's masterpiece of a biscuit. I can't describe how incredible it tastes.

1886 Café and Bakery's Jalapeno Corn Biscuits

Step 1
2 pounds ½ oz all-purpose flour
8 ¾ ounces corn meal
3 ¾ ounces sugar
½ ounce baking soda
¼ ounce baking powder
¼ ounce salt
¼ ounce dry mustard
½ ounce ancho chili powder
1 pound cold butter, cut into small pieces

Step 2

2 teaspoons yeast
¼ cup water

Step 3

3 cups buttermilk
2 eggs beaten
1/3 cup fresh jalapenos, finely chopped

Preheat oven to 350F

Combine all dry ingredients together in step #1; then cut butter into the dry ingredients by slowly incorporating the butter with your hand until all the butter is combined.

Mix the yeast and water together for step #2.

Finally, combine the dry ingredient/butter mixture with the buttermilk mixture, and then add the yeast water and stir in jalapenos until just combined.

Roll out dough, and cut into biscuits. Place on a greased sheet pan, and bake at 350 for 8 –12 minutes or until golden brown and crisp.

Chorizo Sausage Gravy

2 pounds of Chorizo sausage
1 pound breakfast sausage, cooked and ground
½ pound butter
all-purpose flour to form roux
1 gallon heavy cream
salt and pepper to taste

In a large sauce pan brown the chorizo and the breakfast sausage. Add the butter, and cook for one minute. Stir in the flour to form a roux. Cook the roux over low heat for 10 minutes. Be sure not to brown the roux; you want a light-colored gravy. Add the half and half, and bring to a boil. Cook for five minutes at a very low simmer.

Threadgill's World Headquarters Restaurant
301 West Riverside Drive
Austin, Texas 78704
Hours: Mon.–Thu. 11 a.m.–10 p.m.
Fri.–Sat. 11 a.m.–10:30 p.m.
Sunday Gospel Brunch 10 a.m. – 1 p.m. dinner - 9:30 p.m.
(512) 472-9304
Biscuits served for Sunday Gospel Brunch

Southern food, music, friendly service, and plenty of biscuits is what this legendary South Austin restaurant is all about. Locals love the biscuits and massive chicken fried steak served from Threadgill's kitchen. Music and homestyle food go together during the popular Sunday gospel brunch. The buffet is brimming with Southern favorites; biscuits and cream gravy, sausage, bacon, garlic grits, Mexican egg dishes, pancakes, and French toast.

Biscuits and gravy are always homemade at Threadgill's. The biscuit maker kindly shares how it's done.

Biscuit Advice: rotate your biscuit pan halfway during baking to ensure even browning of biscuits.

Threadgill's Biscuits Mix   (they start with this)

1 lb. unbleached flour
3 tablespoons sugar
1 teaspoon baking soda
1 teaspoon salt
2 tablespoons baking powder

Combine ingredients in a large bowl, and mix thoroughly.

Threadgill's Buttermilk Biscuits

3 1/3 cups of flour mix (from recipe above)
1 ¼ cups buttermilk
3 tablespoons whipping cream
¼ cup melted vegetable shortening
3 tablespoons melted margarine
2 tablespoons melted butter

Preheat oven to 350F.

Combine the buttermilk, cream, melted shortening, and margarine. Put the biscuit mix in a mixing bowl and gently mix the wet and dry ingredients together until you have sticky ball of dough.

On a lightly floured surface, roll or pat the dough in a rectangle of about ½ inch thick and cut with a 3-inch biscuit cutter or glass.

Place biscuits on a flat pan lined with parchment and bake at 350 for about 20 minutes.

Cream Gravy   *(big batch)*

4 pounds beef bones with marrow
1 cup vegetable oil and bone grease
1 cup flour
2 quarts milk, room temperature
2 teaspoons Worcestershire sauce
2 teaspoons Tabasco sauce
2 teaspoons black pepper
salt to taste

Roux: Brown the bones in a 400 degree oven for 2 hours. Remove the marrow and reserve. Use grease from bones and enough oil to make one cup. Put flour and oil into a cast iron skillet over medium heat and cook until mixture is the color of butterscotch, about 8 minutes; stir constantly. Don't scorch the flour.

Gravy: Add room temperature milk slowly, whisking thoroughly to avoid scorching. Add Worcestershire, Tabasco, and black pepper. Cook until milk is absorbed into roux and thickens to your liking. Salt and season.

Houston

The Breakfast Klub
3711 Travis Street
Houston, TX
Hours Mon. – Fri. 7 a.m.–2 p.m. Sat. 8 a.m. – 2 p.m.
(713) 528-8561
Biscuits served all hours

It's breakfast call in Houston and time to flock to The Breakfast Klub. The place is packed with a line out the door for helpings of the Davis family's biscuits, gravy, fried catfish, grits, and famous waffle/wing breakfast combo. This is the place to get your biscuit fix. The Breakfast Klub has a homey atmosphere and a "you're part of the family" feel to it. Gospel music plays in the background competing with the clanking of dishes and lively conversation.

Constantly voted Houston's "Best Breakfast," Chef Anthony declined to share his tried and true biscuit recipe or any other recipe for that matter. You have to love the message on the restaurant answering machine, "If breakfast is the most important meal of the day, why not have it twice?"

Lankford Grocery And Market
88 Dennis Street
Houston, Texas 77006
(713) 522-9555
Hours: Monday – Saturday 7a.m. – 7 p.m.
Biscuits Saturday Breakfast only

Eydie Pryor, owner of the Lankford Grocery and Market, serves up Texas charm and hospitality at her neighborhood restaurant. Eydie's parents bought the grocery in 1939 and in 1977 Eydie transformed the store into a charming eatery that the locals love. Eggs and homemade hash browns are breakfast favorites with burgers bringing in the lunchtime crowd. Biscuits and cream gravy make Saturday breakfast at the Lankford Grocery and Market special. Eydie says her homemade biscuits are time consuming, so she only breaks out her rolling pin for that one day. Her biscuits are light and fluffy and always served with her famous white pepper cream gravy. Eydie is one of a "no measuring cup" type, so there are no exact measurements for her biscuit recipe. Eydie's biscuits are simple, made with all purpose flour, lard, and whole milk. The crowning glory she says is the pepper gravy.

Biscuit Advice: top any biscuit with cream gravy and you have a winner.

Eydie's White Cream Pepper Gravy

all-purpose flour
milk
butter
salt
pepper

In a skillet, mix butter and flour to form a roux. Add milk, and stir until the mixture thickens. Salt to taste; then add a lot of black pepper. Serve with homemade biscuits.

Mama's Café
6019 Westheimer Road
Houston, Texas 77057-4501
Hours: Mon. – Wed. 6:30 a.m. – 2 a.m.
Thursday – Friday 6:30 a.m. – 4:00 a.m.
Saturday 8 a.m. – 4:00 a.m.
Sunday 8 a.m. – 2 a.m.
(713) 266-8514
Biscuits served for breakfast

Take a trip down memory lane while you eat big biscuits and breakfast at Mama's Café in Houston. Old matchbooks, movie posters, and other antique collectables hang on the walls of this Texas comfort food favorite. Bert and Felix are the biscuit makers here. They bake about one thousand Texas-sized biscuits every week that are served with country skillet egg dishes. A house favorite is Huevo's Hofbrau; scrambled eggs with hot chili, pico de gallo, chili con queso, and German hash browns. This spicy concoction is served with biscuits and sausage gravy.

Mama's does burn the midnight oil with breakfast served as late as 4 a.m. on weekends. Like most of our Texas restaurants, Mama's doesn't give out the biscuit recipe but will share these biscuit making tips.

Biscuit Advice: Bert and Felix prefer to use baking powder with buttermilk over baking soda. They believe the soda/buttermilk combination makes biscuits rise too fast and they may fall. They also think baking soda is too salty. Mama's biscuits are also topped with real butter.

Triple A Restaurant

2526 Airline Drive
Houston, TX 77009
Hours: Mon. – Fri. 5 a.m. – 8 p.m.,
Sat. 6 a.m. – 3 p.m.
(713) 861-3422
Biscuits for breakfast

The Triple A Restaurant is rolling in the dough; biscuit dough, dumpling dough, and pie crusts. Everything is homemade at this home-style restaurant which has been serving it up fresh to Houstonians since 1939. Biscuits are served at breakfast, topped with gravy and pan sausage. The sausage is ground and seasoned in the Triple A kitchen.

The diner is owned by the Schmidt family which claims that anyone can serve a frozen biscuit—so why? Homemade buttermilk biscuits, chicken and dumplings, and an array of fresh vegetables bought daily at the neighboring farmer's market are always on the menu.

Cecil and Janet Schmidt won't give out their exact biscuit recipe, but they make their biscuits with flour, baking powder, sugar, salt, and a mixture of buttermilk and whole milk. Breakfast at the Triple A is staggered throughout the day. You can get breakfast at from 6 a.m. to 11 a.m. - with lunch served until 2 p.m. - then breakfast is offered again until closing.

Marble Falls

Blue Bonnet Café
211 Hwy 281
Marble Falls, Texas 78654
Hours: Mon.-Thurs. 6 a.m.-8 p.m.
Fri. - Sat. 6 a.m.-9 p.m.
Sun. 6 a.m. - 1:45 p.m.
(830) 693-2444
Biscuits served till they run out

The Blue Bonnet Café in Marble Falls, Texas, serves square crusty biscuits with cream pepper gravy. The biscuits go perfect with the Blue Bonnet chicken fried steak for breakfast. This Texas Hill Country café serves its satisfying biscuits and breakfast all day. Regulars and visitors have been bellying up to the counter of this quaint diner since it opened in 1929.

The buttermilk biscuits are big, square, and crusty outside and tender inside. Owners John and Belinda Kemper are always on hand to work the cash register or to make biscuits. They say the biscuit recipe is the same today as the day the café opened. No telling here, just easy tips on how to make your biscuits square.

Biscuit Advice: Belinda says, "After you roll your dough out, cut the biscuits with a round cutter and place them so close together on the pan that they push into each other and turn square when they're baked!"

The Blue Bonnet Café in Marble Fall

Blacksburg

Famous Anthony's
1353 South Main Street
Blacksburg, Virginia 24060
Hours: Monday – Thursday 6 a.m. to 10 p.m.
Friday & Saturday 6 a.m. – 10 p.m.
Sunday 7 a.m. – 10 p.m.
(540) 961-7600
Biscuits served for breakfast

Famous Anthony's professes to be the main biscuit joint in Blacksburg, Virginia. William Webb, manager and biscuit maker, says the restaurant bakes about four thousand fresh biscuits a week. Famous Anthony's is often voted the "best breakfast" in town and serves biscuits, gravy, and grits with its breakfast specials. Webb says when Famous Anthony's franchised, switching to frozen biscuits was considered. That idea was nixed with the realization that frozen biscuits were not as good the homemade biscuits his customers had come to expect.

Biscuit Advice: Work fast -- Mix the dough and get the biscuits into the oven; don't let trays of biscuits sit around – they'll go flat.

Famous Anthony's Biscuits

4 cups self-rising flour
½ teaspoon salt
1 teaspoon sugar
½ cup shortening
1 ½ cups buttermilk

Heat oven to 400F.

Cut shortening into dry ingredients. Add buttermilk, and roll out. Cut with 3-inch cutter for nice big biscuits. Bake at 400 degrees for 10-to12 minutes.

(There are 10 Famous Anthony's)

Roanoke

The Roanoker Restaurant
2522 Colonial Avenue Southwest
Roanoke, Virginia 24015-3121
Hours Tuesday – Saturday 7 a.m. - 9 p.m.
Sunday 8 a.m. - 9 p.m.
(540) 344-7746
Biscuits served all hours

Fresh biscuits are treated like fresh coffee at the family-owned Roanoker Restaurant in Roanoke, Virginia. Roanoker's biscuit maker bakes country biscuits two dozen at a time, that way they're always served fresh and hot. This is really something, because the restaurant seats 300. The

Warren family says, "biscuits that sit around are like coffee left on the burner, no good." Customers are used to being told, "It will be three more minutes until biscuits!" The country biscuits are served along with corn sticks and yeast rolls, all part of the come cooking coming from the Roanoker kitchen.

Fresh biscuits have been a key part of the restaurant's reputation since it opened in 1941 as a small downtown diner. The Warrens make it a priority to keep the biscuits and home cooked meals just as good as when they were served out of the original small kitchen.

The Warrens make their flour mixture up in big batches. They cut the shortening into the flour and store it and use it as they need to make biscuits. They simply add the baking powder and buttermilk to the pre-made flour mixture to quickly make their biscuits.

Biscuit Advice: E. C. Warren says, "It's a mistake to think that by adding more baking power or baking soda that your biscuits will rise better. It actually makes them rise and then collapse."

"Making good biscuits take nothing more than patience and practice, practice, practice."

Williamsburg

Old Chickahominy House

1211 Jamestown Road
Williamsburg, Virginia 23185
Hours: Weekdays 8:30 a.m. – 2:30 p.m.
(757) 229-4689
Biscuits served for breakfast

   The Old Chickahominy house is a local and passersby favorite in Southern Williamsburg. Thinly-sliced Virginia salt cured ham served on square biscuits is the unique offering at the Old Chickahominy House. What keeps diners coming back for more is the tasty combination of slivered ham on the thin crisp biscuits. This colonial style restaurant is a mile-and-a-half from the historic downtown Williamsburg. Beautiful antique furniture and architectural elements add to the historic feel of the 1962 restaurant. Plantation breakfasts include Virginia ham, grits, eggs, cured country bacon, and the square biscuits. At lunch chicken and dumplings and Brunswick stew are served along with homemade buttermilk, coconut, and chocolate pies.

The Old Chickahominy biscuit recipe belongs to Melinda Henderson, who cuts her biscuit dough into squares after rolling. She says this method is fast and eliminates the re-rolling process. Here's how the Chickahominy House baker makes the biscuits.

Biscuit Advice: Square biscuits are different and that makes them real attention getters and you don't waste the dough.

For a thin biscuit, roll the dough to a ¼ inch thickness. The taste of flavorful hams and meats can be experienced better on a thin biscuit.

The Old Chickahominy House looks like home. Many say it's like having Grandma cook breakfast.

The very Old Chickahominy's square flat biscuits go perfectly with Virginia salt cured ham.

141

Old Chickahominy House Biscuits

2 cups flour
½ teaspoon baking powder
½ teaspoon baking soda
pinch of salt
4 tablespoons lard
1 cup buttermilk

Preheat oven 400F

Combine dry ingredients, cut in lard, and then add
buttermilk. Combine to form a dough ball. Turn dough out
onto a lightly floured surface, and roll out ¼ inch thin. With
a large sharp knife, cut dough into squares like a sheet cake.
Bake for 10 -12 minutes. Biscuits will be thin and crisp.
Don't leave them in too long, or they'll be like crackers.

Pass the Ham Ma'am

If air could be tasted it would be now. Not just tasted.
Throw in sliced, savored and devoured. I share my thoughts
as I breathe in my surroundings. For I sit in the most unusual
yet appropriate place to write to you about country ham. A
Tennessee ham house. Above me hang 5-thousand salt cured
hams doing their time. For that's what a country ham does.
Time equals taste.

Ed Rice in front of his Country Ham Store in Mt. Juliet.

I sense history in the soul of this dark space. A place where
the Southern time-honored tradition of curing ham survives.
Here, suspended golden brown hams age for up to a year.
They dangle off the sides of the old brick and wooden walls,
in every nook and cranny—even high from the rafters. Hog

heaven. To me, what I see looming above are 5-thousand special memories waiting to happen. In the South, country ham makes a celebrated appearance at special occasions; Thanksgiving, Christmas, Easter, weddings—you name it. The country ham's most expected and classic attire is to arrive at these events dressed in a Southern biscuit. The ham biscuit. Or the ham and biscuit combination—a match made in culinary heaven. The rich salty flavor of the country ham is counterbalanced by the starch of the biscuit. Some butter their ham biscuit. Others dip their ham biscuit in red eye gravy. One Southern girlfriend of mine slathers on strawberry jam. She says the salty ham, sweet jam, and biscuit are the perfect combination. Hmm, that one I've got to try. There's a good humored age old argument over which came first, the country ham or the Southern biscuit? Each, is arguably a cornerstone of Southern fare. Yet, no matter how you slice it—country ham is the salt of the South.

Inside a traditional country ham house.

The Skinny on Country Ham

Curing Country ham like baking Southern biscuits is a dying art. Fewer and fewer people do it because it each takes time and effort. For those who are unfamiliar; the country ham is like a fine cheese or a great bottle of wine. There's an art and science to the process. It is somewhat complicated. Confusing—especially if you've never heard of country ham or had it prepared the right way. When I've witnessed people eating country ham prepared correctly, they often say, "This is not too salty like the country ham I've had before."

Cold hams are packed in salt and stacked. It takes about a month for the salt to absorb into the ham before they're safe to wash, dry and hang in the ham house to cure.

Yes, country ham is cured in salt. If you don't prepare it right it can taste like playdough. It is just like serving a good Bordeaux before the bottle is given the proper time to breathe. Same difference. A bad outcome. But if done properly—a fantastic epicurean payoff.

So let's start with; what is a country ham? Most country hams come from Virginia, Tennessee, Kentucky, North Carolina and Missouri. The country ham cut comes from the rear leg of the pig.

The country ham, like the biscuit, can have differences in taste depending on the recipe, or ham curing process. Country ham can be cured in different combinations of salt, sugar and spices and dry aged for varying time periods ranging from three months to a year or two. Some hams are smoked, others are not. Hams up North, referred to as "city hams" actually have water put into them to make them moist and heavy. Country ham curing takes the moisture out as it dry ages. A 25 pound ham that is cured for a year will weigh 17 pounds on average when it is prime for the picking. That is why the meat is dense, rich, dark velvet and flavorful.

Country Ham Homage

Country ham dates back to the days of colonial homesteading. Like churned butter and beaten biscuits, country ham was born out of necessity. Making the most of ones resources. Food for survival. Curing was a method used to preserve meat for the year using nature's refrigeration. Back then, a hog was slaughtered at the time of year when a month or two of temperatures below 40 degrees were guaranteed. That length of time was needed for the salt curing to preserve the ham for safe aging during higher temperatures of the aging process. So, the first two crucial steps in the process; starting with a ham that is freshly slaughtered and cold. The meat must be cold, below 40 degrees. The ham is covered in the curing salt mixture and needs to absorb the mixture for about 40 days, again in that below 40 degree temperature. After that, the ham is washed, bagged and hung in a dry place where it dry-ages. At that point the ham is safe from spoilage as long as the ham house is properly ventilated, warding off moisture. Some curers smoke the hams for flavor during the aging process.

Country Ham How

I've been given country hams before I knew much about them. It can be intimidating. It's a thing of beauty and you know it is a prize -but then what do you do with it? To start with, be thankful you have one; you're in for a treat. Then, think ahead. Act a few days before you want to serve the ham. What you need to do is basically rehydrate the ham, which adds moisture and extracts the salt. I've read countless recipes, but basically depending how salty you like your ham, wash and then soak the ham in cool water for at least a day switching out the water. Some, including myself, soak the ham for two to three days. One country ham lover advises to soak your ham in an ice chest type cooler so you can control the temperature, keeping it at the magic 40 degrees. Switch the water out as you see fit, but at least every 12 hours.

Now that your ham is rehydrated you have options. Some boil the ham in on the stove in a brine of peppercorns, bay leaves, bourbon, onion and spices (20-25 minutes per pound) then keep it in the fridge to slice off of for up to three months. You can also take the boiled ham and trim and score it, placing cloves on the ham and roasting it at 400 degrees for 15 minutes to brown, keeping internal temperature at 160 degrees. Others smoke the ham, or slice, fry and grill it. A most popular option is to pour Dr Pepper, 7-up, or Coca Cola over the sliced or baking ham to counterbalance the saltiness.

A side note, most country ham operations I've visited now sell sliced country ham vacuum sealed for smaller portions. I love this and use those slices to make country ham biscuits all the time. I soak the ham slices in water for a few hours in a Pyrex dish, switching the water out. Then I fry the ham slow and use the fat drippings in my biscuits. I also brush the tops of my biscuits with the ham fat as well. Also, most country ham operations sell their own unique bacon and sausage, another wonderful Southern find.

Biscuit Tricks

Here's a compilation of the tricks of the trade from our biscuit makers. Glance down the list to find hints that will help you become your own unique biscuit maker.

*Add baking soda to the buttermilk and let it stand for a minute before combining with flour. This is a great way to ensure the leavening agent gets activated and evenly distributed throughout the biscuit dough by way of the liquid.
~ *Phila Hach*

*Don't overwork the biscuit dough. Don't knead it or fold it too much. Handling the dough overworks the gluten or protein in the flour and can make your biscuits heavy.
~ *The Flying Biscuit Cafe*

*If you want crisp biscuits - use a pan with no sides or edges. If you want a soft biscuit - do the opposite.
~ *Buns on the Run*

*Rotate your pan half way during baking to make sure your biscuits bake evenly.
~ *Bryant's*

*Use your fingertips to work lard or butter into the flour. Palms have more heat and soften the fat, leaving you with a flat biscuit.
~ *Martha Stamps*

*Use heavy cream as your liquid if you want your biscuits to keep for many hours before you serve them. Use buttermilk when you're going to serve them right away.
~ *Martha Stamps*

*Cold chunks of butter or lard left in eraser-sized pieces in the dough will make your biscuits fluffy. If you want this effect, chill the lard, butter, or shortening so it doesn't break down.
~ *Martha Stamps*

*Some biscuit makers swear by speed. Make biscuits fast so the baking soda doesn't fizzle out. That means don't let them sit around on the pan before baking. Mix, roll, cut and slide them into a hot oven as fast as possible.
~ *Famous Anthony's*

*Make homemade baking powder to eliminate the metallic taste of commercial baking powder by mixing 2 parts cream of tartar with one parts each of baking soda and cornstartch.
~ *Thumbs Up & Watershed*

*Bake your biscuits alone in the oven. Sharing the oven could mean a transfer of moisture that puts condensation on the biscuits.
~ *Buns on the Run*

*Add spices, dried fruit, or diced meat to your standard biscuit recipe, and you'll have a new version of your standard biscuit.
~ *1886 Bakery and Café & Merridees*

*Always mix all your dry ingredients together before adding the fat and liquid. If you forget something like baking powder and add it later – flatsville!
~ *The Beautiful*

*Add flour into the liquid portion of the recipe instead of pouring the liquid into the flour mixture. This way you can control the consistency of your dough better.
~ *Louie's Café*

*Place your biscuits close together on the pan and they will touch and rise higher than if they were placed far apart.
~ *Monmouth Plantation*

*If you like crisp biscuits finish them off under the broiler.
~ *Bryant's*

*Some biscuit makers use combinations of like ingredients to get a unique tasting biscuit. Mix margarine with butter and lard for the fat. Combine buttermilk with whole milk or heavy cream for the liquid portion of the recipe.
~ *Barksdale's*

*Mix a combination winter wheat flour with rye, oats, and whole wheat flour for a healthful biscuit.
~ *Thumbs up and Crescent Moon Café*

Eliminate the traditional biscuit cutter by cutting the dough into squares with a butcher knife. There's no waste of dough and no waste of time.
~ *The Chickahominy House*

*Pierce holes in the dough with a fork before cutting into rounds. This allows for even baking and gives biscuits an old- fashioned look.
~ *Watershed*

*Eliminate the rolling out step by making a giant drop biscuit. Just spread mixed dough onto a cookie sheet, score it with a pastry cutter and it's in perfect squares when it comes out of the oven.
~ *Lynn's Paradise Café*

*To get unique biscuits, hand roll your biscuits by pinching off a piece of dough and rolling it into a ball then flattening it with the palm of your hand. No two biscuits look alike.
~ *Mammies Kitchen Biscuits & Mrs. Wilkes Dining Room*

*If you want white biscuits—use whole milk not buttermilk.
~ *Mr. Biscuit*

*While rolling dough, keep it moist on the inside and lightly floured on top.
~ *Pastries a Go Go*

*Brush the tops of your biscuits with real butter. Add garlic, if you wish.
~ *The Lady & Son's & Paradise Café*

*Try European margarine, a blend of butter and margarine, for a better tasting biscuit.
~ *Thumbs Up*

*Don't re-roll your dough; it makes the second batch of biscuits tougher. Bake stray pieces that can't be cut into rounds for interesting shapes.
~ *Watershed*

*Don't twist your biscuit cutter. Go up and down so your biscuits rise real high.
~ *The Flying Biscuit & Watershed*

*Don't "fiddle" with the dough. Make the biscuits fast and get them into the oven faster.
~ *Lilly's*

*Pat your dough into a disc; rolling it with a rolling pin is "violent" and stretches and tears the top layer of dough.
~ *Louie's Cafe*

*Cut biscuits small, about 1½ inches round for a petite ladylike biscuit.
~ *The Carriage House & Martha's at the Plantation*

*Keep your biscuit dough mixture cool by putting shortening or lard in the freezer before adding to the flour mixture.
~ *Monmouth Plantation*

*If you use lard, use a high grade filtered hog lard. It should be pure white. Lower grade lard is yellow and stringy and will compromise the taste of your biscuit.
~ *The Beacon Light*

*For crispy flavorful biscuits, brush the bottom of your pan with melted lard, and brush the tops of uncooked biscuits with melted lard as well.
~ *The Beacon Light*

*Light-colored baking pans mean light biscuit bottoms. Dark pans turn the biscuit bottoms dark.
~ *Barksdale's*

*If you put sugar in your biscuit mix, bake biscuits at a lower temperature to keep the sugar from browning. This makes sugar biscuits nice and white.
~ *Blue Plate Café*

*Mix two Southern favorites for a great biscuit- cornmeal and flour.
~ *Miss Mary Bobo's*

*If you don't have any buttermilk on hand, make your own by adding ½ teaspoon of vinegar with whole milk.
~ *Monell's*

*Fold in whipped egg whites to make your dough light and reduce the need to use baking powder.
~ *1886 Café and Bakery*

*Make your biscuits turn out square by placing round cut biscuits so they're touching on all sides on the pan. When they bake and expand, they take on a square-like shape.
~ *Blue Bonnet Cafe*

*If you plan to put meat on your biscuit, like ham, roll the biscuits out thin, ¼ inch thick, so you taste more of the meat and less of the biscuit.
~ *Chickahominy House*

*Refrigerate all of your ingredients, even the flour, before making your biscuits. This keeps the dough chilled even in the heat of the summer. Your biscuits will be all the taller and lighter.
~ *Poogan's Porch*

*Biscuit dough should be wet, almost "tacky," to produce a soft biscuit.
~ *Hominy Grill*

*Don't twist your biscuit cutter – it will crimp the edges of the raw biscuit, making it only rise in the middle after baking. For an even taller biscuit, go up and down.
~ *The Early Girl*

Author's Notes

To my Readers with Love,

I'm coming clean. I never baked a homemade biscuit until I completed the documentary, **The Rise of the Southern Biscuit.** Prior to the documentary, I thought biscuits were picked off a tree in a pop-open can. I am reformed. Through my work I have found my own biscuit religion. I am like many of you, a biscuit maker in the making. I've seen it all and tasted it all and I've attempted it all. My biscuit baking journey continues as I learn something every time I bake. But here's what I've got and I hope it helps.

My Biscuit Kitchen

*I use the recipes and biscuit tips in the book as a guide. I measure with my hands. I aspire to be like Phila Hach, my biscuit mentor. You can see her approach in the bonus footage in **The Rise of the Southern Biscuit** or by going to **www.theriseofthesouthernbiscuit.com**

*I found it takes making biscuits time and time again to get it down. But once you've got, you've got it. Experiment and keep track of what works. Mix in the same order, use the same pan, pay attention to the flour and ingredients you're using, and the temperature of the oven.

*Know your oven. Baking time depends on your oven for all recipes. I've learned that high heat is best for me. I bake my biscuits at 450 degrees. I brush the tops with butter and brown them by turning my broiler on low to finish them.

* Flour. I use plain soft winter wheat flour. I don't use all purpose or self rising flours. I add my own baking powder and baking soda, salt, and sugar. Why? Because, I've been known to keep the same bag of flour for a long time and the leavening agents do lose their rising power.

*The fun of biscuit making for me is tradition. I like using my favorite large wooden "biscuit bowl" to mix my dough. I use my husband's grandmother's sherry glass as my biscuit cutter and her antique sifter to combine my flour, salt, baking powder, and sugar. I bought my wooden rolling pin on a special vacation. So my biscuit utensils are special to me and the love transfers.

*Control the mess. Baking biscuits can be very messy and that could keep you from wanting to make them. The idea is to get it down quick and easy. I place my bag of flour in one side of the sink, my large sifter in the other side. I scoop my flour into the sifter, add my salt, sugar and baking powder and stir it in the sifter: then sift into my large wooden bowl. I've gotten pretty good at keeping the biggest mess to a flour spot on the counter where I roll my biscuits, which really doesn't have to be that much flour (forget what you see in the movies and on TV)

*Don't overdo anything. When using recipes in the book: add liquid a little at a time and mix your dough. I have made the mistake of adding in all the suggested liquid and it being far too much. When that happens add more flour to make it balance. Also, I've given into the temptation to add more fat thinking my biscuits will taste better. All that does is weigh the biscuit down.

Maple Bacon Biscuits

Who doesn't like bacon and who doesn't like biscuits? So I had the idea to do a bacon wrapped biscuit. I was telling friends about my vision and got two great suggestions: wrap the bacon around the biscuit like a little filet and add maple syrup as great contrast to the bacon. So I did.

Maryann's Bacon Biscuits

Here's how I do it: I line each space in my popover pan with par cooked center cut thick bacon. I stuff my biscuit dough in the middle. Brush with butter and bake in a 450 degree oven for about 12 to 15 minutes. I brown the tops with my broiler. The bacon turns out crisp and wonderful. I pour maple syrup on a plate and place the biscuits in the puddle so the syrup absorbs into the biscuit bottoms. You can drizzle some on top as well. I think they're pretty fabulous.

Wedding Cake Biscuits

I love my little wedding cake-like biscuits. Reminds me of my Mother, Carol Byrd, who baked and decorated wedding cakes as a side job from our kitchen when I was little. I loved to watch her stack each layer and I think that's where the inspiration for my hallmark biscuit comes from. I like my biscuits to look like a celebration.

So this is my trick to make a tall biscuit with ease. Stack layers and—poof!—*tall* biscuits. They're special looking and I enjoy putting different themes together. I do them in two and three tiers. Stack two rounds, the bottom bigger than the second; and then I use tiny cookie cutters to place a third. I use my heart shaped cookie cutter most.

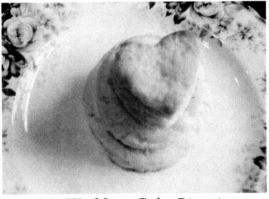

My Wedding Cake Biscuits

I really enjoy baking biscuits and genuinely believe that biscuits are memory makers. I hope all of you find your biscuit groove and I hope the book serves more as inspiration in helping and you come up with your own biscuit tradition.

Love & Biscuits,

Maryann Byrd

159

Alphabetical Listing

CPSIA information can be obtained at www.ICGtesting.com
229406LV00001B/2/P